An Esthetician's Guide to Growing a Successful Skincare Career

Douglas Preston

wishing you the best
of success !

Dedicated to you

TABLE of CONTENTS

Introduction

In 1982 I began my career as a professional esthetician with only one goal in mind. I was determined to make a living doing what I loved before being forced to quit to do something I probably wouldn't like as much.

I knew little about the practice of skincare in those early days. To complicate matters I knew even less about what it would take to earn a living and turn the choice I had made into a thriving career.

Still, I was determined to make a go of it, especially after having witnessed many of my co-beauty students drop out of the profession due to disappointing results or because they never put their license and skills to good use. In fact all I really knew for certain was:

- I didn't have much time before I needed to start making some money,
- I was nervous, doubtful and pretty close to being broke,
- I was afraid to fail in my profession,
- I had no clue how long it should take to develop a good customer clientele,
- I had no money for marketing (there was no internet yet!) and,
- I didn't know where to turn for sound advice.

My many doubts and fears made my goals all the harder to believe in. I knew I didn't have the luxury to just sit around to see how everything would turn out. I needed to do everything and anything to find and please skincare clients so they would keep coming back.

This seemed like an almost impossible task. Worse yet, 1982 was a recession year and professional esthetics was a fairly young industry in the United States. For working estheticians, there just didn't seem to be enough regular customers to go around.

Perhaps the worst things I struggled with were the continuous scary thoughts that constantly swirled around in my mind during those many empty hours and days at my little skincare clinic. Thoughts like: "Will I ever succeed in this profession? Is this career right for a man? If I fail, what will I do?" My confidence was drained, which made a tough situation even tougher.

Day after day the phone refused to ring, the door almost never opened and my schedule looked like a volunteer signup sheet for a public flogging — no one was on it! After two months I had barely made enough money to buy gas to drive to the shop. The third month proved even worse than the first two. I came close to locking the door and giving up. There was no one around who seemed to have experience in starting a new esthetics business and no mentor to turn to for help or reassurance. I was completely on my own…fortunately you don't have to be.

Despite facing those challenging conditions, I doggedly pursued my career in professional esthetics which ultimately led to spa ownership, becoming a business consultant, a well-respected authority in professional skincare and the author of this book.

The content on these pages is intended for present and future spa or esthetics professionals—anyone else willing to work hard in turning their career choice into a reality in spite of potential worries that can make success seem quite uncertain.

This is not just a business story, rather, it is a valuable guided tour through the forest of questions and decisions you will encounter as you make your way toward a satisfying profession. The better equipped you are for the journey, both mentally and technically, the easier it will be for you to bravely conquer the obstacles all career people encounter on the path to achievement.

This book will prove to be your best friend on dark days, a voice of calm and reason when anxiety invades your thoughts, and a valuable, reliable manual for making wise decisions in building and maintaining your skincare practice.

My several decades in business can now serve as your own personal instructor in the art of career success. We can also make the growth of a skincare practice light, fun and not such a serious experience! Being able to laugh at myself and at all the silly, embarrassing and just plain dumb ideas I have had over the years was a huge part of the strength I needed to get ahead.

Please take your time reading through these chapters. Stop to think carefully about the perspectives and methods you'll discover. Allow yourself the patience and self-care needed to turn learning into skill.

This book is as much about the power of the mind as it is about putting ideas into action. Both are required in quality and consistency to realize positive results. We're not talking about miracles here, but a timeless way of doing and being applied to anything in life worth the effort.

Now, I do ask one thing of you. If you experience personal growth by putting to use the principals outlined in this book, please share your progress with co-professionals either by teaching them the skills you've developed or by suggesting they obtain a copy of this book for themselves. What is good for one is often good for all, so please pass it along!

My best to you,

Douglas Preston

1 What is a Professional Esthetician?

Is it possible that you've come all this way through your career or beauty school program without ever clearly knowing exactly what it means to be an esthetician?

That may be true if you define your profession by the offerings on your service menu: facial treatments, medical aesthetics, body waxing, makeup application, etc. But the skincare professional, at least from the client's perspective, is much more than a person performing personal services.

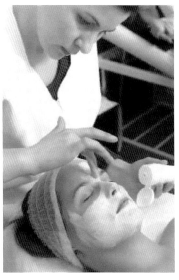

A moderate to high degree of intimacy and trust often develops between a service provider and client, one that can deepen and expand over years of professional/ client contact.

In helping you to understand the responsibility and sensitivity in client interactions, it's useful to have some insight into how esthetic professionals are viewed by those who patronize them.

Decades of treating women, men and teens in a private setting has gifted me with an astonishing "insiders" access to the hidden lives of people being people; contemplating and doing things that others who are more familiar with them could possibly find suspect, out of character or even shocking. Their personal revelations can be told to you as casually as describing a television show. Expect the unexpected!

The Esthetician as a Skincare Professional

Far more than just a service provider working in a treatment room, a skincare professional is someone who can deliver useful advice and education literally anywhere she or he goes.

Whether you're attending a party, seated in an airplane or standing in a supermarket line — the skincare professional is someone who is equipped with a special knowledge and understanding that can have a profound impact on the feelings and appearance of others; something almost everyone is interested in learning how to improve.

You are someone possessing the power to positively and permanently change lives whether that change is measured in an enhanced personal satisfaction or an elevated self-esteem.

No matter where you go you are prepared to perform a valuable service for others. This broad definition of a working esthetician opens the door for you to earn money in a large variety of settings, something we'll discuss later in this book.

Once, while waiting in a coffee house line, I saw a mother standing in front of her teenage daughter; the daughter whose face was plagued with inflamed acne was glumly staring at the floor, disengaged from any of the people around her. Seeing this, I quietly spoke to the mother and told her that I could correct her daughter's skin without the use of medication. I handed her my card, offering a free acne consultation. She brought her daughter to me almost immediately and soon we were well on the way to eliminating an embarrassing and painful problem for a vulnerable schoolgirl.

You can imagine how gratifying that was for everyone involved, not to mention a good business technique for the ambitious esthetics professional. Even if this assistance hadn't led to an appointment we can still have the wonderful self-satisfaction of knowing that somehow we've attempted to make a positive difference in someone's life.

The Esthetician as a Friend

Over the years of skincare service many of my clients have become long-time personal friends. These friendships naturally evolved out of certain commonalities in background, humor and experiences that made deep bonds almost impossible to deny. I've attended weddings, funerals, anniversaries and birthday parties, even family events such as Thanksgiving and Christmas dinners. Some of these people can be counted among my very best of friends.

More often the friendships you develop with special clients exist in the salon or spa setting only; a sort of long continuous reunion which includes a running story of your lives, loves and other special events. My longest client relationship is now going on 36-years; someone I've seen through many of her working years and now well into retirement. As a woman in her early 80's I don't see her quite as often as I once did, but she is still a loyal client and a cherished friend.

These client friendships need not include off-site get-togethers or personal phone calls. Facebook has proven that the idea of friendship can simply be expressed through small comments of appreciation and gestures of approval. As a busy, work-driven society we've steadily come to conduct friendships by means far more convenient than spending hard-to-find time together. While not everyone we define as a friend will be the one we can call on for support when a serious personal challenge arrives in our lives, they can still be pleasant sources of interaction, wisdom, feedback and fun. It's important to understand the difference between casual/professional friendships and those where deep personal sharing and responsibility are included. There can be a fine line between casual and serious relationships and not everyone is skilled in knowing or respecting the difference. Also, an employer may have certain rules related to client and employee interaction, both verbally and physically. It's important to honor the rules of the house when working for someone else.

When clients are also our personal friends, questions in regard to charging them a fee for professional services can become uncomfortable. In such situations is it still appropriate for you to bill them for your time and work? If you do charge them, should they be expected to pay the same rate as someone you consider a client only? You may not want to have many client friendships if you allow them to cost you money.

My policy has always been that except for rare instances of need, I always fully charged client friends for the services they schedule with me. This eliminates any misunderstandings and assumptions that can lead to hurt feelings or resentment. It's never cost me a real friend! If you wouldn't go to your friend's workplace and make them work for you without compensation then you need not allow it in your place of business either. Any respectful friend will understand and honor this reasonable policy.

The Esthetician as a Confidant

This one is a bit harder to handle as it can involve serious personal subjects you may neither want nor feel qualified to hear. Without any reservations whatsoever clients have showered me with stories ranging from disclosure of mental problems, romantic affairs, animosity toward family members, to criminal acts. Often clients have told me stories they wouldn't dare tell their therapists. Sometimes it can seem as if they

4

really have no one else to talk to about certain things that are fascinating or troubling to them. This can lead to trouble for you, too. In my early years as an esthetician I confess that it was an honor to be trusted by clients to the point that some of them would share truly personal stories with me. But, what I didn't know was that a number of these people would become sort of addicted to this act of sharing, and a few of them began to visit or call me at the spa in between appointments with updates or "emergencies." This I didn't want and was unprepared to deal with, especially for fear of losing the client if I didn't accommodate their emotional needs.

I learned that there is a big difference between listening and engaging, and I recommend stopping at listening, only as a means of escaping interactive obligations. It's also useful to know the difference between offering perspective and casting an opinion (also known as judgment). Perspective involves possible interpretations of any given situation whereas opinion suggests a black and white statement about the way something is. So, when a client asks, in the middle of a relaxing facial, "Do you think he's cheating on me?" Respond with the possibility that he's stressed out, distracted or overworked. Then return to the business at hand.

I made the mistake once of backing a very loyal client in her outrage over her unfaithful husband. It was the classic story of catching him fooling around with an office co-worker and being in complete denial about it. My client told me she was leaving her husband and would never give him a chance to hurt her again. Trying to be supportive and thoughtful I agreed that leaving the cheating mate was probably the best thing she could do, and be glad to be rid of him. But, three weeks later she took her hubby back in and, humiliated to face me with that not-so-admirable fact, stopped coming in to see me. It was a lesson well learned and expensively earned.

One esthetician I mentored explained how she permitted a client friend to "temporarily" move into her apartment after the client lost her job. Two months later not only did the friend still live with her, but the friend's new guy was making regular visits at night— not exactly a comfortable situation for the host when the friend was sleeping on the living room sofa. Worse still, the friend could no longer afford to pay for facial treatments but was now receiving them for free while living rent-free with her esthetician! Not having the courage to boot her guest out of the house created an unhappy and costly situation that seemed out of my mentoring client's control.

It's difficult to say exactly where you may want to set your personal and professional limit with clients. A good place to start is to take an honest look at your own personality and values. If you're the sort of person who has difficulty setting boundaries with people or feel guilty about taking money from friends then it might be a good idea to keep your client relationships more to the business side. This way you'll avoid the trap of losing money and professional freedom when your heart speaks louder than your wallet.

Remember, your profession comes first as does your commitment to yourself and your own wellbeing. You have an ever present obligation to love and care for yourself, the person who is always there when no one else is present. Unless you care for yourself first you won't have the energy or strength to help someone else. Sometimes caring can mean not offering assistance to another because it can, in fact, turn into something even more harmful than the immediate problem. It's what flight attendants instruct passengers related to emergency procedures. "Adjust your own oxygen mask before assisting others." You can't help someone else breathe if you aren't able to breathe yourself.

Finally, The Esthetician as a Businessperson

I've never met a skincare professional whose main goal in the career was to run a business. But, whether we like it or not, the managing of our business will turn out to be the most important item on our list of daily duties.

By business I'm referring to just about everything that happens before and after performing a treatment. These tasks at hand represent the majority of what we do in a working day. Even if you work for someone else, there are plenty of non-treatment responsibilities that go into building and maintaining a skincare practice. Here's apartial list:

- Facility Maintenance
- Cleaning
- Laundry
- Tax Records
- Accounts Payable
- Bookkeeping
- Insurance and Licensing
- Banking
- Marketing
- Printing
- Client Record Keeping
- Scheduling
- Appointment Confirmation Calls
- Inventory Ordering
- Product Sales

Exciting, huh? I know you can't wait to get started on your every dayor few times a week "to do" list! If you decide to become an employerthis list will grow far larger with additional duties. It's even worse ifyou're not so good at handling them, as many of us are not (why didwe choose this profession, anyway? Not because we're accountants or business geniuses!)

Most skincare professionals find themselves forced to deal with the details of business just to do what they really want to do — practice esthetics. Needless to say, the business side of the career might not prove to be the most functional part of it! You could hire a business manager but don't forget: someone has to manage the manager and that person will be you. There's no escaping at least some involvement with the business side of your practice, and you'll need some skill there, too.

But, unless you dream of launching the next big thing in multiple location skincare centers or even running a single large and busy one, you can get by comfortably with only a handful of expert guidance and a little more consistency. I am far from your classic business wizard, but I still managed a few happy successes in the field of professional esthetics, and you can too!

NOTES / COMMENTS:

1) What discoveries did you make while reading this chapter?

2) How will you use the information you learned?

3) List 3 things you will do to advance your career.

2 How to Plan Your Career in Professional Esthetics

Congratulations! You may now find yourself well on your way to becoming a licensed esthetician. Or perhaps you're newly licensed or… you've been working in the professionfor some time, years perhaps. Regardless of where you currently find yourself, thereis an important question you should be asking yourself, "What kind of esthetics career is the right one for me?"

It's interesting to note that for the majority of esthetics students and those who have graduated and are now working; most had little or no knowledge about their ideal working situation or what kind of long-term career result would best suit them. For the majority of working estheticians, it seems that only two things matter most; to get licensed and to find employment.

But first let's consider these statistics: most licensed estheticians remain in the business less than five years before abandoning it while many who remain struggle to earn a sustainable living. With that in mind, now is a good time to begin thinking about planning your career. Here are some questions I often ask new estheticians, including typical responses to them:

Q: What is the goal for your new profession?
    A: I want to be busy.

Q: Ok, how busy?
    A: What do you mean?

Q: Well, how many hours a week do you plan to work?
    A: I don't know, full-time I guess.

Q: By full-time do you mean at least 40-hours per week?
    A: I'm not sure. I need to make money right away and I also have a child, husband, dog, cat [or whatever] to take care of.

Q: How much money will you need to earn then?
    A: I really don't know yet.

Q: How much money do you think you can earn performing esthetic treatments?
    A: I don't know.

Q: Let's assume you're already busy with a full day of appointments. Would that make you feel good?
    A: Yes!

Q: Ok, you're busy, but doing what?
    A: I don't understand what you mean.

Q: What if you're fully scheduled doing bikini waxes all day long. Would that be ideal for you?
    A: Well no, not really.

Q: Then what would your ideal appointment day look like?
    A: I don't know, maybe a mix of things - facials and waxing I guess.

Do you see a problem in that conversation? It appears that many new skincare professionals have almost no idea what should be or needs to be done to become financially stable. This is also one of the most common reasons so few ever financially succeed in an esthetics practice.

Having a vague idea about money, working hours, a compatible salon environment or what it actually takes to become "busy" are concerns that need to be asked and accurately answered. It's simple: if you don't have a plan of action, then you don't really have a plan. So if that's the problem, what's the solution?

This chapter is designed to help you decide which career path best matches your interests, your available time and work habits, your personal preferences regarding occupational environment, and also understanding the income you'll need from your job as quickly as possible.

This doesn't involve work that requires a graduate degree in business; rather, it's just a simple process of self-examination. Ask yourself the questions and record the answers that reflect your sincere professional desires, needs and true capabilities. Anything else is unrealistic and potentially costly.

When I first started out as a licensed esthetician I, along with so many others, didn't have a clue about what this profession would be like, what it would demand of me. I had no real concept of how much money I could earn doing whatever it was I would be doing, and certainly no clear thoughts about the kind of esthetics career I would or even could have. I, too, just wanted a full schedule of...um ...something.

Mostly I was terrified that nothing would come of my career. And nothing was exactly what I had achieved outside of becoming licensed. It was then that I realized that I had a problem, and understood that I needed a plan.

It's important to note that a career plan, no matter how well thought out and detailed, never actually leads to the outcome it was designed for. Why? Because opportunities, new interests, adjustments in the economy and many more unexpected influences change the plan you first envisioned. That's just a part of life and it's unavoidable, yet might possibly offer something better.

Many of the professional benefits I have enjoyed during my years in esthetics have come from ideas and sources far different than those I first conceived. Now as I look back on that original plan, I can also see just how narrowly it was defined because of being based on all that I knew at the time I crafted it. How thankful I am today that I kept an open mind!

In order to help you develop your own business plan I have created a list of employment options that will probably include some that you will most likely choose either at the beginning of or sometime during your career.

Each option will have features you may find attractive and realistic, while others may not seem so appealing. Be honest with yourself when considering them. Don't exaggerate what you know to be the truth about your habits, preferences and abilities. Avoid creating a reality that isn't actually there. Reaching for higher goals has always been a great idea. But if you're going to need a ladder to get there, make sure you have the ladder first instead of committing to situations that demand more than who you are or what you have to give.

All of the "You Can Do It!" books and lectures of recent years have led many people to believe that just by wanting something passionately enough, it will somehow magically appear. While you canaccidentally stumble upon the right career choice, making it a reality is going to take smart planning and hard work. So, why not get started?

What's in Your Business Backpack?

Since you're heading into the unknown it is important to be as well prepared as possible for this new adventure. Before moving forward let's see what supplies you already have and what requirements your new career will likely demand of you.

Work Availability:
- Are you able to commit to 40-hours (or more) of employment per week?
- Do you prefer a part-time position?
- How far are you willing to commute to a workplace?
- Are you familiar with traffic patterns that may affect your commute?
- Can you or are you willing to attend company meetings and training sessions during odd hours or on your day off?
- Are you flexible with regard to working hours and days?

Reliability: (Be extremely honest with yourself here)
- Are you a true on-time person or do you often tend to run late?
- Are you forgetful or do you remember every detail?
- Does your personal life or second job make it difficult to maintain a set schedule?
- Do you experience frequent personal emergencies, drive a car that's on its last leg, have children or others in your life who regularly need your assistance on a moment's notice?
- Do you tend to "bite off more than you can chew" or over-commit to people and situations?

Capabilities:
- Are you a fearless self-promoter and sales person or do you dislike the idea and act of selling?

- Do you consider yourself more reserved or outgoing?
- Are you a fast learner or do you need extra time to master a skill?
- Do you enjoy reading training materials?
- Do you easily adapt to sudden change?
- Do those with superior skills or titles intimidate you?
- Are you a natural leader, a follower, or do you just prefer to fit in with others?
- Do you consider yourself open to new ideas and expectations?
- Are you headstrong and stubborn or more compliant?
- Are you highly skilled and experienced in your profession or in need of more training and practice?

Income:

- How much money do you minimally need to earn in order to stay in whatever esthetics job you take?
- How soon will you need to make that amount of money?
- What can or will you do (in addition to your esthetics job) to supplement your income if necessary?
- Who can or will help you if financial assistance is required?

I also feel that commitment is equally as significant as the other personal qualities I have listed, but I do want to discuss it separately because it is perhaps the most important strength you can possess when trying to start a new career.

Without a true, burning commitment to achieving a satisfying and financially rewarding esthetics career you won't have the ability or patience to wait out the early months, maybe years of slow growth, inadequate pay and circling self-doubt that nearly all new professionals in any field experience.

Lack of dedication is probably the main reason most newly licensed estheticians fail to stay in this career; finding the work or the need for more money so challenging that they don't stick with it. There is no shame in discovering this in yourself. The main thing is to give your profession all you have and then be honest about your feelings throughout the journey.

If you make it as a professional esthetician then congratulations to you! If you change your mind about it then a whole new world is still available. You'll know what to do.

Now a few words about "passion." So often, whether in job interviews or mentoring meetings, I hear estheticians describe their passion for skincare as the reason for choosing a career in esthetics, the reflection of a burning desire to help others and to do something meaningful for a living.

Yet, for the majority of them, that passion blows out as fast as a birthday candle when the harder unforeseen realities of the profession begin to appear. It's important not to mistake mere interest for passion. Passion is emotional fire, or as one dictionary defines it, "an intense desire or enthusiasm for something."

Passion is what makes artists endure poverty in order to create. It's the drive that compels people to risk their lives to climb dangerous mountains. Passion is what keeps us in love despite the challenges of being in a relationship. It's behind what you want so badly you'll do almost anything to have it. True passion doesn't fade away as easily as simple desire.

It's the passion found in Shakespeare's story of Romeo and Juliette. It's this kind of passion, real passion, that will carry you through your esthetics career from beginning to end.

Even now, after thirty-five plus years of professional skincare work, I stillhave as much or even more passion for what I do than I did when I first started. Passion gave me this unimaginably enjoyable career and it'swhat led to the writing of this book.

Firmly dedicate yourself to your skincare profession and give it everything you've got. Just know that those who entered the profession only to vacate it later will have helped to clear the path before you. Stay with it, work hard, love your clients, and you'll receive many wonderful rewards!

Planning Your Work in Esthetics

There's a song in the movie, "The Rocky Horror Picture Show," with a line that says, "Don't dream it, be it." I agree that while it's important to dream, which is the same as imagining, that dream will need to become a set of instructions for actions you must take in order for the dream to ever become a reality. That means having a plan in place that you understand and are committed to (yes, commitment again!). Most estheticians have only a loose plan or none at all other than finding work in the field. While that's a reasonable start, it's not likely going to lead you to who you really want to become. This next section is all about discovering just what "becoming" is for you.

What Kind of Esthetician Will You Be?

At the beginning of your career you'll probably be happy just to land a job doing almost any kind of esthetics work: facial treatments, body waxing, possibly makeup (whatever comes along that can fill your schedule and produce income). But later, after you've performed your millionth Brazilian or shaped countless eyebrows, you may feel that you want to become more focused on a certain area of esthetics work that's more interesting, easy to upsell and offers the best opportunity for retail sales.

what are
your
dreams?

When looking at the average daily appointment schedule, it's usually filled with a random mix of services, but mostly waxing in the beginning and sometimes wellinto one's career. Now there's nothing at all wrong with waxing, especially if that's what you truly enjoy doing, but let's consider the full working opportunity of the professional esthetician.

The reason why most esthetic schedules develop the way they do (filledwith a hodge-podge of services) has more to do with chance ratherthan any decision or planning on the part of the esthetician. It's what I call a "whatever" schedule, meaning, it reflects whatever business happens to call in, come along or what one has been doing in the past provided it's been done well enough.

Since most new future appointment business will come from past client word-of-mouth referrals, the services you've been performing all along will represent most of what you'll be referred to do for others. So if, for example, waxing is what you mostly do now, then waxing will likely be what clients ask for most often in days to come. Will you really look forward to doing a full leg and bikini wax at the end of a long, tiring day?

Your career will grow from the seeds of what you've been planting. The question is, what will bring you the most income and opportunity? Let's work that out here.

Your Ideal Day in a Skincare Practice

Imagine if every day, before leaving work, you could simply fill in whatever kind of appointments you wanted for the next day and they would automatically be there. How amazing would that be? Is it possible to accomplish such a thing? Yes, it is, especially if you are focused on what you want and use every working opportunity towards achieving that goal. But, before you do that, let's see what might be the most personally and financially rewarding for you as a skincare professional. We will start by evaluating the productivity of each main type of service an esthetician performs with regard to upselling, up-grading, retail sales and referrals.

- **Waxing/Sugaring:** A potentially higher ticket appointment with relatively low cost to the esthetician. But, except for facial waxing, this is a more physically demanding service than many of the others. It may not be that easy to upgrade this treatment since most customers know what they want to do when they come in, and adding additional wax areas may require you to include extra time which you may not have available. What about retail sales? How likely are you to sell a product to your client related to the service of waxing? If your goal is to turn the waxing client into a future facial client, how effective do you think you'll be in successfully promoting such services to her?

- **Makeup Application:** Is this a plentiful client in a spa or salon? Can you easily upgrade the service? Retail sales may be easier with this type of customer than clients those receiving waxing or sugaring, but how effective are you (or think you are) in selling the makeup you're using during the appointment? Is this customer one who is easily converted to facials or waxing? Is makeup a service you'll frequently receive referrals for?

- **Facial Treatments:** Could this treatment be upgraded during the assigned appointment time (special masks, peels, serums, etc.)? Is it a difficult treatment to perform back-to-back as opposed to waxing and makeup where you'll be on your feet most of the time? Is it a higher-priced treatment from the start? What sort of retail opportunity (commission!) does the facial client present to you? Would you anticipate more referrals for your facial services?

Looking at each of the services individually you already see that facial treatments are the most financially lucrative and physically comfortable services on your menu of options. Facial treatments  are an easy upgrade with facial waxing, home care product sales and even makeup as all are beauty related. So ask yourself what sort of career experience you would most enjoy. What services would give you the greatest personal satisfaction? All of these details should be considered when making important decisions about your career.

Attracting More of Your Ideal Customers

Without having to write an entire book on marketing, let alone a separate chapter, here is a potent fact to remember about marketing. What you talk about the most regarding your profession, and the services you most frequently perform are what others will most likely hear about from your present clients. And what the public learns about you is both what they will probably come to you for and then recommend to their contacts as well. Knowing this, what will be your primary service story?

For example, in 2011 when I opened Preston Skin Center in San Jose, my initial goal was to be the premier anti-aging skincare destination in Silicon Valley. While I steadily grew business in that area, I soon recognized that Groupon, Living Social and other discount deals were thinning the ranks of available facial customers willing to pay full price. Because being a discount skincare center was not a part of my plan, I needed a strategy to deal with competitive pressure coming from estheticians that were trying to win customers on the basis of price alone. I quickly saw that by resetting my focus on non-medical teenage acne treatments (something you have to be very good at in order to grow that clientele), I could attract and keep these special clients without the need to discount them. In fact, deep discounting can often cause a concerned mother or father to suspect that your services may not be the most effective for their child.

Preston Skin Center is now the go-to clinic for acne control services with a large loyal following besides my anti-aging offerings. Word-of-mouth referrals among local families, schools and even physicians have been tremendous. The acne focus has attracted skincare business for children of moms and dads who would normally not use my services, sometimes adding a son or daughter to a facial care program one or both parents already receive from me.

While treatment upgrade opportunities and retail sales are somewhat more limited with acne clients than those receiving anti-aging services, the sheer volume of acne business more than makes up for it. I still get plenty of anti-aging customers but the hot talk is about my acne work… and where there's talk there's business!

So, the challenge for you is to decide what your service specialty will be and then keep your customer and contact talk focused on whatever it is that will best lead to your goal. That means limiting the subject to one or two closely related services at most!

At a recent local business networking meeting one of the new members stood up to introduce herself to the group and to tell us about her company. She began by saying she had a mobile notary office that offered clients the option of conducting their notary transactions at a convenient location of their choosing. Okay good, something unusual and easy to remember. But then she went on to describe no less than a dozen other completely unrelated services she also performed, annoying the group with forgettable and time consuming "focuses" that made her sound more like an incompetent and confused person than a professional one could feel confident in. She ruined her credibility in this best chance to leave a good impression with referral peers.

Narrowing your career focus doesn't mean that you won't attract business for your other esthetic treatments. But, it does present an idea of you as someone who is a true specialist in something both desirable and easy to recall when people talk about you, talk that shouldn't involve a long list or a lot of time. You can promote a larger array of options after you win the customer. What you're looking for is a referral spoken like this: "You must go to Kristin for facial peels. She's absolutely the best and her treatments just make my skin glow!"

Simple, enthusiastic and easy to remember!

NOTES / COMMENTS:

1) What discoveries did you make while reading this chapter?

2) How will you use the information you learned?

3) List 3 things you will do to advance your career.

3 What You May Not Have Learned in Beauty School

Possibly the most valuable skill any skincare professional can acquire is the deep and sensitive understanding of how clients think and feel when in our presence and under our care. As much as we may feel we know what clients want, there is likely  a whole world of perceptions and preferences that can easily go unnoticed or unexpressed. These hidden realities are oftentimes the primary ones clients use to judge our professionalism or our treatment results.

Customers are generally very reluctant to tell their esthetician about something they don't like, especially while or immediately after experiencing it. Most prefer to be polite. They may behave as if satisfied with our work and even leave a gratuity while, in fact, they're actually dissatisfied with the service they just received. It's only later, either by never seeing the customer again or through feedback that came from a Yelp review, or a comment from another customer, that we discover our service was a letdown. By that time it may be too late to do anything constructive to correct the problem.

Maybe we've all experienced poor service somewhere ourselves and failed to make our feelings known to those who could do something resolve a situation. I once had a massage in a large Las Vegas resort spa that bragged about having recently spent millions of dollars in a major remodel. I think they should have devoted some of that money to staff training, especially in regards to customer service skills.

My massage treatment was performed by a technician with inappropriately long fingernails that drove painfully into my back with each stroke of her hands. I finally informed her that I was uncomfortable (as if my rigid, arching back wasn't evidence enough) and asked her to avoid dragging her nails across my skin. She responded with, "Oh, okay." She then finished the treatment by barely touching me. The whole experience was ridiculous. I ended up paying the ticket and even leaving a tip. When the front desk person asked me how I liked my massage I told her exactly how it went. Not being properly trained in what to do in such cases she said, "Um, well, we won't charge you for the service then." But, while she deducted the charge for the massage, she retained the tip!

When spa and salon personnel think of their own priorities over that of their customers, their work is bound to suffer or fail. Offended clients can and do get their "ounce of flesh" out of an unapologetic business in many creative ways, not the least of which may include talking negatively about the poor service to family, friends, co-workers, neighbors and anyone else who will listen to them or read their complaint online. If a client is upset enough they'll embellish the story too: "She practically tried to kill me during that facial!!!"

How Skincare Customers View the Esthetician

One reason estheticians so often misread their clients is because they are never skincare clients themselves. If you have had facial treatments in the past as a licensed esthetician your present perception of that experience can have a huge influence on your work.

Simply said, estheticians are often not the most qualified people to understand what the client is thinking and feeling while performing their treatments. Clients are not experienced estheticians, and do not judge our work from a deep technical knowledge of the service. They largely evaluate us by how they *feel* when receiving a professional treatment.

With their eyes closed, and drifting into profound relaxation, they don't pay great attention to the steps that make up the facial treatment they're receiving. Some even fall asleep. So there's little chance the client will have an expert way to rate your treatment against one they had in the past. Most clients are passive and compliant, ready and willing to be led by the skilled technician to do what they were hired to do.

Never forget the credibility an esthetics license assigns to the skincare professional. We're educated and highly trained experts trusted to know our business the same as physicians, CPAs and airline pilots are considered experts in their chosen field.

Clients do not make appointments with skincare professionals they don't believe they can have faith in, though certainly that faith can be lost through poor service or treatment results. I can think of only a few people out of many thousands who have questioned my qualifications or methods prior to a facial or other treatment. While some professionals have more experience in a career than others, it is naturally assumed that anyone working in a licensed position has the skill to fulfill its demands.

We are in a profession that's admired and one we can be proud of. In fact, some of my own clients are or plan to become estheticians, receiving services from me in order to glean some additional education from their appointments. They represent some of my favorite customers because I can help demonstrate a well-practiced example of how a top-level skincare professional handles clients, and how a deep knowledge regarding methods for solving problems with the skin is a tremendous benefit to our clients.

But, not every esthetician exhibits strong professional standards. Running late on appointments, rushing clients, paying little attention to client needs or comfort—any of these can diminished the reputation of beauty professionals in the eyes of customers.

Television, movies and the media often portray beauticians as flaky, dumb and/or comical --- think of Gilligan's Island Day Spa. Sadly, there are plenty of service providers who behave so badly that these perceptions are lent some legitimacy. A smart esthetician will know this and do everything possible to appear a superior standout in the esteem of customers. And it's so easy to do!

Types and Characteristics of Skincare Clients
One of the greatest benefits in working with skincare clients is the opportunity it provides for learning about people. Understanding the various personality types, sensitivities, and wisdom gathered from our experiences is offered to us through stories and personal expressions revealed in an environment of trust and privacy.

After a number of years in the profession we come to see certain consistencies in customers and, while not wanting to stereotype individuals, some aspects of values and behavior become strikingly familiar to us. Learning to recognize varying kinds of clients and having a reasonably accurate idea about their way of relating to the service professional can bring some real advantages to your efforts in selling to and retaining them.

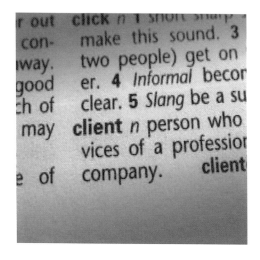

To begin this, I'll list my rating system for customer types in terms of their value to your practice. Please note that this is not intended as a means of judging human-beings personally (we love and respect all of our customers), but when looking for the best opportunity for building business and deciding how to market your services, a little background on how people often interact with a skincare professional is very helpful.

By the way, when I list a gender preference in my customer ratings it is not with the intention of excluding anyone. The purpose is to identify your best service and retail sales opportunities, along with new client referral potential, per customer type. Your marketing dollars and efforts will be best invested in attracting customers who are most likely to add significant growth to your business.

The "A+" List Client
A female who found you on her own or through a referral and didn't use a gift certificate to pay for your services. "A+" list clients range anywhere from late 20's to early 60's, have aging or acne concerns (or both!), and are often career women.

The "A+" list client visits regularly, rarely forgets or misses an appointment, is open to your treatment suggestions, buys lots of retail products and refers like crazy. She's positive, works and lives locally, is always happy, makes you feel better after you've treated her. She also tips generously! You'll find her easy to please, forgiving and someone who will likely become a years-long client. This is your absolute best customer and you want as many of her as you can find.

The "A" List Client
She's any new female customer very similar to the "A+" list client with a few exceptions. The "A" list client doesn't visit as often as an "A+" or spend as much on retail products. But, she's reliable, refers friends, and will use other services on occasion. Job commitments and/or family obligations can and often do interfere with the "A" list client's commitment to a steady routine of skincare or waxing appointments.

Another "A" list client is the teenage acne client. While she or he may not purchase a wide range of products or upgrades, you can count on frequent visits and lots of referrals from happy parents if your treatments achieve positive results. Because teenage acne treatments may be scheduled often and are sometimes viewed as "clinical," paying parents may not be as inclined to leave gratuities. I never show the gratuity feature to acne clients on my point-of-sale system as I prefer for them to regard me more as a health care provider, enhancing my professional image among them.

The "B+" List Client
This client can be either male or female, a local but irregular visitor with some or no retail purchases and limited concerns about their skin's appearance. Relaxation is probably the biggest benefit of the facial treatments they receive. The "B+" list client refers few if any new clients.

If the "B+" list client is a male he will not be as likely to upgrade to waxing services nor be inclined to purchase makeup. He isn't likely to refer other men, but may introduce a female friend or spouse. By the way, men are ideal gift certificate buyers!

The "B" List Client

While the "B" list clients are very similar to "B+" list clients, they will most likely see you because of having received a gift certificate for the visit. You may be able to convert them to a "B+" list client, but most will either wait to receive another gift certificate before they return, or not come back for a long time if at all. Still, it's good to have local people who have used and value your services, possibly recommending you to others. B-listers are also occasional visitors who call at the last minute to schedule an appointment. While infrequent customers, as you gather more of these over the years of practice they will represent an important schedule filler you can rely on.

The "C" List Client

She or he is a one-time visitor usually taking advantage of a gift certificate, raffle prize or discount special you may have offered at your business. This is likely a "feel-good" customer only and less inclined to purchase retail than most, though such sales are not out of the question.

Hotel spa clients often fall into this category. If building a steady clientele is your aim, the "C" list client will probably not do much to help you with that. Like "B" customers, C's" are useful for "filler" appointments in that they do fatten your salon schedule even if they're constantly changing faces.

Finally, the "D" List Customer

During your career you'll mostly meet wonderful clients who are a pleasure to work with and make your service days a pure joy. But as we all know, the world is made up of a great variety of people and personalities. Enter the "D" list customer. I refer to the "D" as customer only and not client, because turning one into a client is either impossible or undesirable.

"D" customers are often gloomy, picky, hard to please, frequently late for or forever changing their appointments. They are also often unapologetic about no-shows. This individual likes to return treatment products that are half-used due to unexplained "reactions." They may also ask numerous questions about self-care advice yet express discomfort with some of your treatment methods. You can never feel confident that you've satisfied the "D" customer, even if she or he reschedules with you.

The "D" list customer can leave you feeling exhausted, insecure or insulted. The good news is that they will prove to be quite rare in your practice and will usually move on to another victim before long. On a more positive note, the "D" list customer can bring you valuable opportunities to learn about handling difficult behavior.

The bottom line is that anyone who comes to see you is a whole person deserving of the best of your skills and hospitality regardless of her or his unique characteristics. It is you who will need to conform to the varying needs of clients, not the other way around. You will learn to do this skillfully and confidently over years of practice. These experiences are a valuable gift you'll use again and again throughout your career.

When Customers Disappear

One day a wonderful client you've seen for years suddenly drops off your schedule. It's almost as if Thanksgiving Day is missing from the calendar, so reliable was your customer. This can be a disturbing realization both personally and financially. Your mind begins to consider all of the possible reasons why this "regular" client has vanished. Did you do something wrong during the last visit? Did she find someone she likes better? Has a Groupon or other discount offer won her away from you?

If you're like most skincare professionals the idea of directly contacting one of these missing clients makes your blood run cold. What if she's angry with you or has passed away?

Clients occasionally fall off your "regulars" list for reasons that only pause their loyalty to you, not end it. Family vacations, holidays, a brief illness or a heavy business travel schedule can interrupt a reliable treatment routine between you and your client. As busy as people are these days, they do not always remember to get back on board with past routines once the ability to do so returns. Sometimes they just forget. It's circumstances like these that make contacting the absent client worth the effort.

Nevertheless, you still may not be comfortable calling a missing client. I'm not asking you to change your personality or feelings about that now, but even sending a reminder card with a little special incentive can do wonders to revive missing clients. We learned a long time ago of the need to remind customers of their scheduled appointments. This has had the unfortunate result of many clients not bothering to remember an appointment at all unless reminded by our courtesy call. After all, if someone is willing to perform a task for you why bother to do it yourself?

Highly demanding lives can require certain obligations such as prescheduled skincare appointments to be brought back to our client's radar screen. We certainly don't want to lose business to a customer who fails to show up for a valuable piece of our workday. This is one way automated scheduling systems (with automatic client reminders) really pay off!

How to Handle No-Shows and Last Minute Cancellations
This never-to-be-completely-avoided experience is one of the most irritating, expensive and demoralizing for every esthetician or appointment dependent professional. From restaurant reservations to surgery, meetings with an interior decorator to

a date in traffic court, people forget, lose, ignore or cannot keep their scheduled appointments on any given day no matter what. The customer reserves your time and then fails to appear or reschedules her appointment for another time. It begins to feel as if money is being stolen directly from your wallet, and you become insulted that anyone could be so inconsiderate of you.

Your mind wanders through a series of unhealthy fantasies: a certain client is rude and thoughtless, people are no good, you'll never make it as an esthetician, and so forth. This sort of thinking depresses your mood and casts a dark shadow on your outlook, even your self-esteem. These lost appointments are especially hard for the new skincare professional who is looking forward to that one facial treatment on the schedule and who really needs the money it may have earned.

Okay, just the mention of these experiences has probably made you feel a little tense. Here's what I want to tell you about this: no-shows and last-minute cancellations are a fact of professional life. No policy or penalty will ever fully rid you of this unpleasant reality. They will never stop completely and there's nothing much you can do about them except to send reminder notices a day or two before the appointment. Let's be absolutely honest about this, have you honored every appointment and obligation you've made in your life? I doubt it and know that I have been guilty of it more than once in the past. Somewhere someone was unhappy with me over that act, unintended as it was.

Life simply isn't as ideal as we would like it to be, nor does it always cooperate with our needs or expectations. On the very last day of your skincare career with 40-years of loyal customer service and the best reputation in your area, when flowers and balloons fill the salon honoring your tremendous success and retirement, someone on your schedule that day may fail to show up or call to reschedule. That's why we must make every appointment count!

Knowing that your client day could shrink unpredictably you'll wantto maximize the value potential of the appointments you do service eachday. Focus on what you have, not on what you were hoping for. The sooner you accept this fact, the sooner you can use the unexpectedopen time constructively; perhaps to do some writing, maybe even send those "I miss you" cards and emails! Try to see this time as an opportunity, not a punishment.

Knowing the Clients You're Looking For (and Finding Them)
Although I briefly addressed this in Chapter 2, it's worth studying more deeply to make sure we don't overlook the importance of it in planning an ideal business future. When you're first starting out in your esthetics career you'll be glad to get almost any kind of customer for whatever type of service she or he wants. You need to build business and earn some money, so you can't afford to be overly selective about what comes along. But, you can begin to shape the direction of your career and the type of client you typically attract and serve by creating a plan for that and sticking to it. No, you don't do this by accepting certain customers and refusing others unless you truly can afford to— that's a good way to starve or lose your job! The strategy is to identify the kind of client you most enjoy working with and who brings you the best business.

In my practice I've selected the "A+" anti-aging and teenage acne "A" clients as my preferred visitors. Here's my reasoning:

- "A+" while being a very valuable client may not always be in ample supply each week. Plus, I like greater variety and purpose in my work.
- Teenage acne clients are interesting to treat, extremely reliable when satisfied with the results, and likely to introduce my services to households that might not otherwise use them. Many a mom who likes seeing her child look and feel better because of my work has chosen to try my anti-aging facials for herself. There are entire families I now serve because of an initial appointment with their acne-affected teenager.

By focusing on these two types of clients I have gained a strong reputation for being an expert in both disciplines, and receive most of my referrals for the services I provide for them. This offers me an excellent customer base with great upgrade possibilities and a lucrative retail trade.

However you market your business, whether it's through print, social networking or casual conversation, you'll be wise to become recognized for a narrow range of services that you're especially talented in.

You may do everything within the scope of your esthetician license, but if you're popularly known as the best person to see for microdermabrasion or acne treatments you'll get more value from the marketing buzz you generate. Personally I'm quite competent with makeup design and can shape a mean eyebrow, but I choose not to fill my schedule with those less valuable appointments. While I don't push makeup or brow services in my practice, I'm happily willing to do them upon request.

The downside of specializing in specific service offerings is that it may take you longer to attract and retain a sufficient supply of clients to fill your treatment schedule. This is especially true if you don't focus your marketing in the direction of these unique people. The skincare customer is a rare enough bird to begin with so narrowing your service focus creates a niche customer within a niche customer base.

If the service or services you plan to do have high upgrading and retail potential, plus shorter revisit cycles (such as a peel series), you may see more money from even fewer daily appointments. Remember, patience and commitment are the main keys to succeeding in any sort of esthetics career, but especially so in a specialty practice.

Another potential downside to this plan is the fatigue of repetition. Imagine a day, week or month filled with back-to-back microdermabrasion, peels or acne extraction treatments, or Brazilian waxing from morning to the end of your shift. While being thrilled to have a full schedule of appointments would that kind of routine satisfy you? Service variety is one of the best parts of working in professional esthetics.

I know an esthetician who developed a very successful eyebrow shaping practice; it's virtually all she does her entire day and she never seems to tire of it. She sells makeup, brow colors and brushes along with the brow service and charges premium prices. I could never do that no matter what the financial reward. Switching between acne and anti-aging clients throughout the day offers me the interesting mix of services my mind demands. I admire that professional for her achievement, but she and I are different. What from your understanding of yourself will work best for you?

Where Skincare Customers Are and Aren't
Consider this simple logic: if you want to catch fish you need to go to the lake, not a swimming pool. Just because you happen to be living and licensed in a certain city or town doesn't mean it's the one that will adequately support your career. If your

community has a majority population of more mature adult residents you may not easily attract an acne clientele.

Where retirees make up the majority of the population and fixed incomes are common, your business may not grow quickly. Rural areas with fewer people and possibly lower incomes could slow or limit business. Resort town may not provide reliable local clientele year round. Large, congested cities may pose problems of inconvenience, heavy competition and parking challenges. And even if you're the only esthetician in town, you may not be able to achieve a business the locals are interested in. In other words, don't plant palm trees in Alaska.

I opened my most recent skincare salon in an area of Silicon Valley, California with a known demand for esthetic services. Yes, there were plenty of businesses where one could receive facial treatments, but only a handful of these spas and esthetic salons were highly regarded.

I set my sights on out-shining the best of these by doing what I have always done – providing top-quality skincare treatments with superior client education and genuinely warm and friendly customer service. My salon made the news and my business grew quickly.

You may think that a large metropolis is a perfect place to open a skincare practice. It certainly could be, with a high density and sophisticated population living and working there. But cities often mean steep rents and you serving customers living in a loosely knit community. It may not be easy to circulate your name among those residing closest to your salon.

Another thing: don't count on friends and family to support your practice even though they may swear to before you open for business. It's not that those close to you don't care about you or your career, but sometimes when someone they love is

excited about a new venture they feel compelled to offer
encouragement without genuinely committing to patronize it.

I've heard many estheticians and spa owners bemoan the fact that
they were excited to see their friends among their first customers
after opening a new business only to wonder where they went off to
later. This is the "talk is cheap" factor in action, meaning that it's
easy and inexpensive to say you'll do something, but another
matter when you have to pay for your claims.

Potential skincare clients are literally everywhere. They're at the
gym, your church, in a grocery store line, at a nightclub—virtually
anywhere you go publicly or privately someone is there who is
interested in improving her or his skin. There is no ideal "place" to
find them because anyone could consider your work of real personal
value. To wait for the right time or location to promote yourself is
like looking elsewhere for the wind: all you have to do is run and
you'll find it passing over your face.

Customers are not found while you're sitting in front of the
television. They won't jump out of a magazine or materialize from
your iPod earbuds. You will not find them while sleeping in and
they won't knock on your door while you hide in an empty

treatment room. And even the belief that your social networking site will produce new skincare clients is likely to be disappointing compared to the simple act of being out where people, real live people, can be found.

Living your passion means turning your career into something greater than your work. It means making it a personal mission to bring its people-pleasing power into the lives of others, wherever those others are. And it's as easy as this:

> *"Laura, I work in professional skincare and I am looking for new clients for my practice. If you know anyone who has concerns about skin aging or acne, I would really appreciate it if you would suggest me to them."*

Who would turn down a request as honest and straightforward as that? You give Laura few business cards and thank her for the consideration. That's all there is to it except that you're going to do this dozens and dozens of times during your career. It costs you nothing and builds your true contact network, and it's more productive than typing on your Facebook page. People bring people—how many of them are you approaching each day?

Make "Ask" a Daily Task

The great human potential guru Anthony Robbins taught me this one: "Ask for what you want from those who have it." I first tried this after my bank turned down a request to raise my business's credit line. After reviewing my application the bank officers decided to decline it. Dejected and somewhat miffed that a good customer (me) had been refused more consideration by my bank, I drove home wondering how I could change the outcome of the bank's view of my company.

I had a Robbins CD in my stereo and started to play it. He began to talk about how people were capable of developing the courage to ask for what they want in life. He suggested that if someone declined to give you what you're after, and if your request is reasonable and doable, simply return and ask again. Now that might take more courage than some of us have at present (and was absolutely more than I had then) but I recognized that overcoming the fear to try again might reap substantial rewards.

So, taking this advice I went back to the bank the next day and submitted the very same credit application to the same bank officer. Knowing that committees review these applications I thought it worth a try to see if a different day with possibly different people on the review committee might result in a favorable decision. What did I have to lose even if the bank officer sighed negatively when I asked her to resubmit the credit application?

Two days later the request was approved and the only thing I did was to ask a second time!

By asking for what you want, you make it clear to others exactly what you are looking for and how they can help you get it. In this case I'm referring to new customers. If you engage this "asking" behavior often enough you will soon have a small team of promoters working for you at virtually no cost except, possibly, for a complimentary treatment on occasion.

I have to emphasize this again: the shy and fearful among us will have a very hard time building a successful skincare career.

Nobody but you and I carry the responsibility of growing our business. The salon brochure, spa website or social networking page just isn't going to produce enough clients fast enough to make most estheticians happy or financially secure.

The longer the process takes the more you'll have to deal with gloomy thoughts, self-doubt and a feeble income. So, ask for what you need. Ask your friends, your family, your clients, your co-workers, your doctor or dentist, your personal trainer, your hairstylist, or your vet. Ask anyone who might know people who may need your services. That's a whole lot of people!

And speaking of asking, if you happen to know other esthetic professionals who might benefit from reading this book, please recommend it to them! My thanks to you!

NOTES / COMMENTS:

1) What discoveries did you make while reading this chapter?

2) How will you use the information you learned?

3) List 3 things you will do to advance your career.

4 Choosing a Workplace

One of the most difficult yet important decisions any esthetician will make has to do with finding an ideal place to perform his or her work. There's so much to consider: location, client volume, rate of pay, experience required, available training, opportunities for growth and many other aspects that can influence your decision.

This chapter isn't another "how to" guide on résumé preparation or interviewing tips but one that will give you some solid insights on what to consider or do before scheduling a meeting with the manager of the place where you may want to work.

In order for you to know how to best select a workplace that's right for you, start with a little self-knowledge and use that information as the foundation for making future job decisions.

I've met few professionals who devoted much if any time to this exercise. If they had, their efforts may have helped avoid some unpleasant discoveries once hired by a spa, salon or physician. One employment candidate I interviewed was shocked to learn that she wouldn't automatically earn $50,000 in her first year as a professional esthetician. Where did she get that idea? It came from her dad, who told her that $50K was the minimum she should make in a "respectable" job!

It might have served her far better had she researched the average earnings of an esthetician before choosing to become one. Needless to say she wasn't offered the job, but neither would she have accepted what she perceived as an unreasonably low salary.

Let's begin by studying the most common workplaces where skincare professionals are employed. Each type of service business will have a unique type of client, environment, management structure, compensation program and challenges. Each will require specific skills, both technical and personal, to meet the demands of the job and survive within the facility among its existing staff.

Competent spa or salon hiring managers already know what type of professional is best suited to work in their businesses. They've witnessed who thrives and who fails. But, there's no need for you to experiment with employers if you know what to expect before applying for a position.

On the following pages you'll find a list of venues where skincare professionals often work. I've attempted to describe many of the practical characteristics and employee expectations that each business will require of those working within them... or hoping to one day.

The Day Spa:

This well-known provider of esthetic services has been one of the more commonly sought places for estheticians to find employment. Popular with customers, attractive to gift certificate buyers, and often featuring better appointed and more luxurious facilities than many other skincare businesses, the day spa can be the ideal workplace for the new or seasoned esthetician.

At my own day spa, we sold so many gift certificates that clients were in ready supply as soon as a new recruit was hired and trained. We didn't require our newer estheticians to have a clientele or even much professional experience. What we did look for was positive behavior, reliability and a serious approach to the esthetics career. In most day spas, employees are either compensated on a commission basis or a combination of salary and commission. Renting a space isn't usually a common option.

Day Spa Positives:

- May have an established clientele of regular and gift customers
- Year-round activity, not as seasonally affected as some businesses
- Attractive locations and facilities
- Lots of inter-professional referral potential
- Often more professionally operated than small salons
- May not offer a station rental option so all employees receive an equal earnings opportunity

Potential Day Spa Negatives:

- May expect significant spa-related job experience
- Service packages will demand strict appointment timing
- Some will have significant retail sales expectations
- Could be a competitive environment when numerous estheticians are employed there and are vying for new customers
- May not offer flexible schedules

Full-Service Salon:

These are traditional hair salons that also offer skincare and nail services. Usually the hairstyling area dominates the main working space with other services relegated to smaller areas or individual rooms. Often, these salons will only have one or two estheticians available, thus limiting competition.

Full-Service Salon Positives:

- Frequently offer commissions or rental arrangements
- Potential cross-reference activity with stylist's clients
- Possibly less retail pressure (if retail is difficult for you)
- Scheduling and sometimes cleaning/laundry services are provided by the salon

Potential Full–Service Salon Negatives:

- Busy, noisy, more casual hairstyling environments may not appeal to esthetic clients
- No guarantee that stylists will support your services with their clients
- You may have to provide more of your own product and equipment
- A stylist/owner may not understand your professional needs
- You may feel professionally isolated among a large team of non-esthetics professionals

Dedicated Skincare Clinic:

Most are smaller operations with two to four estheticians working as many rooms. Often dedicated to facial, waxing and makeup services they may include massage therapy or other services that can be performed in a standard facial treatment room.

Dedicated Skincare Clinic Positives:

- Business may be perceived by clients as a superior location for professional facial treatments
- Owner is usually a licensed esthetician who will know your profession fairly well
- Working environment supports the calm and relaxation ideal for skincare work
- Smaller staff may be more cooperative, offer a sense of belonging
- Great learning environment

Potential Dedicated Skincare Clinic Negatives:

- May be a highly competitive workplace where estheticians fight for new customers
- New estheticians may not receive a warm welcome from established ones
- Treatment methods, products and service protocols may be set and rigid, unfamiliar to you
- Owner may be inexperienced and/or poorly skilled in business or personnel management
- Staff client referrals are unlikely

Resort Spa:

Hotels, health resorts, vacation destinations, cruise ships, ski resorts, etc. They are often large operations with a transient clientele and corporate-style management. These spas may feature a variety of treatments ranging from classical to exotic.

Resort Spa Positives

- New hires are often not required to have deep professional experience or established clientele
- Often located in beautiful settings and feature luxurious, well-appointed spa
- May offer salaried positions with benefits
- Management is usually skilled and organized
- Less competition between estheticians for resort customers

Potential Resort Spa Negatives:

- Many resorts have high and low seasons, potentially affecting work earnings
- Most don't have a repeat clientele which may be less satisfying to the esthetician
- Corporate management style may not agree with the professional esthetician
- Significant retail commissions are often difficult to achieve

Health Club:

Fitness centers can range from small private clubs to large family facilities with cafes and beauty services, including massage and skincare. Many are corporate chains while some are independently owned.

Health Club Positives:

- A heavily utilized health club can potentially offer a built in client source
- Possible marketing assistance from club management
- Club may offer membership benefits to in-house beauty service professionals
- Many feature high-end facilities
- 7-day, early to late hour business could accommodate a very flexible work schedule

Potential Health Club Negatives:

- No guarantee club members will convert to skincare clients
- Some offer only rental arrangements to beauty professionals
- Non-member customers may not want to go to a health club for treatments
- Club environment may not suggest or support a relaxing client experience
- Parking at busy health clubs is sometimes challenging

Medi-Spa or Doctor's Office:

Estheticians have more recently become integrated into the staff of plastic surgeons, dermatologists and other health and beauty-related physicians' practices. Doctors often see them as professionals who can complement medical procedures or attract new patients to them. Many estheticians feel that working in a medical environment is an expression of prestige or higher achievement in a skincare career.

Medi-Spa or Doctor's Office Positives:

- Medical aesthetic patients can be ideal clients for the esthetician
- It's an opportunity to work in an extremely professional environment
- May offer salary plus benefits
- An ideal setting for advanced learning
- Some offices offer medical aesthetic procedures to employees at low rates or no-cost

Potential Medi-Spa or Doctor's Office Negatives:

- Can be very demanding and high-pressure workplace
- Physicians will require above average professional performance and reliability
- Many physicians will prefer estheticians with medical esthetics training
- Medical staff may not integrate well with esthetic professionals
- Schedules may not be flexible and clients may decline to include service gratuities

Going Solo:

This wonderful dream of so many career estheticians, having one's own private practice, is an option that should be carefully considered before venturing forward. Pleasant visions and emotions that may come with the idea of working independently can quickly turn dark if financial difficulties and the sheer load of non-service responsibilities weigh-in as they almost certainly will.

Even if you have the funding, the work ethic and business experience to open and manage a small business, I still strongly recommend working for someone else before starting a skincare operation of your own. Use valuable experience to learn from those who have taken this step before you. Listen carefully, observe the emotions and think about the statements made by owners and employees about the business.

Often you will hear complaints about bosses, co-workers and the need for more income in the business. Never fool yourself into thinking that you have the magical answer for all of the problems another business owner has. You may just find yourself creating a whole new set for yourself.

I know of many former independent estheticians who decided to close their skincare businesses and work for someone else, shedding the extra headache and worry about keeping a costly operation running. While that might seem like the obvious choice under those circumstances, and the esthetician may actually find that she makes more money with less work and trouble, that decision, too, can bring about unexpected difficulties. It's not easy to suddenly switch from a truly independent practice to one now integrated into a business owned and directed by someone else.

New location, methods, products, rules, personnel and working under management that may not fit your sense of fairness or expertise can be hard to adjust to. Freedom, even a freedom burdened by loads of responsibility, can for some be preferable to working under a boss in a tightly (or poorly) managed operation.

I'm grateful that I didn't start out my own esthetics career in private practice. My first position was in a small, dimly lit facial room above a hair salon. The second was in a large, glamorous skincare salon in San Francisco that fell to ruin through the financially irresponsible actions of its partners.

It took me a year and a half to go solo. Well equipped with examples of how not to run a business I was still lacking the first-hand experience of being a salon operator, and at the same time a skincare practitioner. Fortunately, I had a great partner who was as dedicated to making the business work as I was. Somehow we managed to get by and gradually began to earn a decent living. Learning, hard work and luck: that was our success formula.

What's the Best Option for You?

Choosing or discovering the ideal workplace is a little bit like finding a compatible relationship — you may meet that perfect someone in a chance encounter, just as you could possibly realize that you're content working in an environment you had never imagined.

Every esthetician I knew then seemed to want employment at the same San Francisco skincare salon I found to be in complete chaos as an employee. From there I went on to succeed by taking over a tiny, barely visible two room skin and make-up studio located in a small affluent town where I hardly knew anyone. But that opportunity is what brought out the best in me both in creativity and the need to quickly learn business management.

To find the place of employment that's best suited for you, it's probably a good idea to first ask yourself the critical questions below:

- Am I comfortable here?
- Do I feel like management supports my needs?
- Are there enough new customers coming in to help me build a clientele?
- Can I survive on my earnings?

The longer you remain in your career the better you'll recognize the difference between questions and worries that arise from doubt and insecurity, and those that are more practical.

For example, when you're the brand new esthetician starting out on your first job, everything about a workplace may seem completely unfamiliar and even threatening: strange co-workers with their different personalities, treatment methods, products and house rules you haven't mastered. Customers who have seen far more experienced skincare professionals before coming to the inexperienced you. All can be frightening and tempt you to negatively judge the spa or salon you're in. I'm not suggesting that you put up with intolerable circumstances forever, but that you use every working opportunity to learn the realities of the skincare business and your ideal place within it.

Allow time to discover whether any uneasy feelings you may have are the result of truly toxic conditions around you or, possibly, that you're just having a normal (even if sometimes unpleasant) adjustment period. Give yourself a chance to settle in and focus on the genuine benefits your job is offering you. There will be plenty of them if even only examples of how not to manage a business or treat employees and customers.

Accept the fact that you need to gain career experience with situations that don't feel so good to you. It's all part of the world of work, growing a career and interacting with people no matter what they're like or where you encounter them.

Often the worst experiences and people ultimately prove to be our best teachers; it's the harder lessons in life that bring us the best education, not the easier ones. The old terms "school of hard knocks" and "paying your dues" do turn out to be true. Learning doesn't always come from classes we love—but wisdom is the result of life tests we take and pass.

Those who give up or walk out simply because something seems really difficult are the ones who will have to repeat these tests or fail altogether. Don't be one of them.

NOTES / COMMENTS:

1) What discoveries did you make while reading this chapter?

2) How will you use the information you learned?

3) List 3 things you will do to advance your career.

5   Skincare Practices and Essentials

If you've ever attended a skincare or spa tradeshow and walked the aisles of vendor booths you may have experienced the thrill from all those product and treatment options on display. It's the Land of Oz -- a magical and mysterious stroll through lanes of wonderful formulas and devices promising to improve your customers' skin and grow your practice.

Then there are the professional classes led by industry experts helping you to advance your skincare techniques and better manage your business.

I'm a huge fan of these events, having spoken at them, hosted them, and always inspired by their energy and the shared enthusiasm of co-estheticians. They are powerful reminders of the importance and  sheer size of our profession, and a great place to make new friends and meet valuable industry experts. But, for those who are new in our profession or may be uncertain about how to remain current and competitive in esthetics, trade events with their overwhelming lures and messages can be confusing, doubt-causing, and a temptation to unwisely invest considerable time and money.

I once consulted for a skincare spa that had a small storeroom full of various treatment machines sitting dusty and unused. Every time the business owner (herself a practicing esthetician), went to a spa trade show she couldn't resist purchasing something that at the moment seemed like it would help make her business better.

Some of that equipment was still under lease payments and there was at least $50,000 of idle hardware stuffed into a closet.

What she would discover when returning to her practice was that new treatments required the esthetician to educate and sell clients on them—something not every skincare professional likes to do or is good at.

Since the salon's customers themselves weren't asking for treatments they knew nothing about, the new technology became neglected and, finally, getting in the way of one working in a small space. So, into storage they went, joining their costly, orphaned sisters. That wasn't a practical way to improve one's business while an excellent way to lose a lot of money.

If you do commit to a new treatment device or take on an extra skincare line and find these additions are selling with customers, does that automatically mean you made a smart choice for your practice? Without going into a long and dull business lesson, I would like to help you understand how to make wise choices for the overall health of your skincare practice. In part, we'll use what I call the "NDB (Need, Doubt or Boredom) Business Decision Method." Prior to any expensive purchasing commitment you will want to make sure you understand exactly what's motivating the desire to do it:

- **Need:** I absolutely know this new thing will improve my practice and I will do everything possible to make it succeed. My business will clearly suffer without it.

- **Doubt:** I'm worried that I'm falling behind others in my profession and maybe some new treatments will help me catch up and be more competitive.

- **Boredom:** I'm just not inspired doing the same facial routines anymore and want something new to restore my enthusiasm.

We'll also look at the financial realities of investing in new products and equipment. To succeed in business it's essential to understand precisely what it will take in terms of sales to recover your investment and profit from your purchase.

Let's consider two different scenarios whereby you as the esthetician (working for yourself or someone else), feels the urge to buy a new treatment machine or skincare product line. You've read the related materials, heard a convincing presentation from a company representative, or a client asked you about it. Not only does the product or technique seem to offer a way to attract more business, but it also sounds like a lot of fun to use.

As your excitement and interest grows, you can easily imagine the satisfaction both you and your clients will feel after experiencing the treatment your new purchase will offer. The more you think about it the more you become convinced that this addition to your present skincare offerings will make a significant positive difference in your daily productivity and earnings. Now, let's look at it more closely:

The item:	Miracle Moisture Maximizer Machine
Client benefits:	Improves skin hydration and smoothness
Your benefits:	Charge more for treatment and attract new clients

Cost of the machine:	$15,000
Cost per treatment:	$15 (machine-related materials only)
Price of service:	$125 - $150 (one hour)

Let's run it through the NDB Method first:

Need: I absolutely know this new purchase will improve my practice and I will do everything possible to make it succeed.

    ___True ___False

Doubt: I'm worried that I'm falling behind others in my profession and maybe some new treatments will help me catch up.

   ___True ___False

Boredom: I'm just not inspired doing the same facial routines anymore and need something new to restore my enthusiasm.

   ___True ___False

If you answered "true" to number one and "false" to numbers two and three, you may... just may... have a case for investing that much money. If you answered "true" to more than one of the evaluation items in the NDB Method you may want to pause before writing a check, borrowing funds or signing a lease contract. $15,000 is A LOT of money! What will it take to recoup your initial investment only? Let's find out.

If you charge $150 per treatment, then logically you'll get your $15,000 back after performing 100 Miracle Moisture Maximizer services. Right?

$$\textbf{\$150 X 100 = \$15,000}$$

But wait... remove $15 from each treatment for product cost; or ($15 x $100) which equals $1500...translating into the need to perform numerous additional treatments to recover the material cost. We would need to perform 100+ treatments to get our money back. Is that correct? Remember, after 110 treatments we still haven't made a profit. In fact we've only recouped our money from the machine purchase. So, unless we sell the machine used, we still haven't generated any profit. And if we sell the machine we only get *some* money back from services that we performed but made nothing on.

What about other costs? Rent, utilities, laundry, phone, advertising, licensing, insurance, additional treatment supplies, cleaning, maintenance of the machine itself, possible interest on

The machine lease and many other expenses? These, too, have to be deducted from the treatment fee before we can apply any money back to the purchase of the machine. How much does that come to per service? Not sure?

Then there's no way to know what you're making per service. Let's suppose that you didn't have the new machine at all, would that fact have prevented you from doing other types of facial treatments you already know how to do and are prepared to offer without adding the additional cost of new technology)? Would your business suffer or even disappear without upgrading to the Miracle Moisture Maximizer?

And another question: are you sincerely prepared to sell possibly hundreds of new and higher cost treatments to clients knowing what you do about your own selling comfort level? You'll find that no matter how excited you feel about a new treatment technique, your customer's knowledge of it will be far behind your own, so you'll need to promote these services aggressively and consistently in order to generate enough client interest to reach your earnings goal. Estheticians and spa owners believe they're making a profit from their equipment investments well before they actually do, and many, if not most, never do.

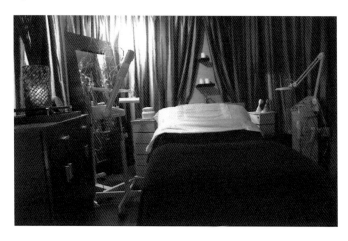

In my own treatment room at Preston Skin Center I only have a few pieces of facial equipment: a steamer, high-frequency unit,

Clarisonic brush, an LED panel, a microdermabrasion machine (not often used because most clients are not ideal for that type of abrasive service), and a single wax heater. And yet my client schedule is booming in a sophisticated area where every sort of skincare technology is available at scores of spas and esthetics clinics. How is this possible?

Am I saying that it's wrong to invest in treatment equipment? Of course not, but I am suggesting that you learn enough about the skincare business to know what you need and what you can pass on in order to succeed.

Manufacturers need you to desire and buy their products — that's how they make their money, and rightfully so. But do you need everything they're selling? Time will help you know whether the addition of costly new equipment, products, or anything that involves money out-of-pocket will result in improved business or profit for you. Until then, take it slow.

Esthetic Practice Essentials
Have you ever known of a hole-in-the-wall restaurant you absolutely loved? Maybe the dining room was small and cramped, possibly the service was less than four-star, and perhaps the location wasn't terribly convenient. But,the food! Because the kitchen delivers the most amazing dishes you absolutely crave, you're willing to put up with all of the shortcomings and inconveniences to dine there.

In fact, sometimes it's a restaurant's deficiency in size and elegance that creates its charm. I've seen these tiny funky places make the unexpected mistake of enlarging and glamorizing to impress customers only to see them disappear as the new décor

Erased the overall experience of the original. The owners made an expensive error in judgment to believe the food was enough to carry the customer over and that the new interior and space would attract and serve more diners. The end result was a shuttered business.

When I owned my first small skincare studio in California, every time we expanded it our most loyal and long-time clients would warn us not to lose our warmth and intimacy. They loved our compact size and the valued familiarity our little facility offered them. But, we grew and grew, and each new expansion brought in customers we never had before while steadily costing us those who had appreciated us for what we were when our relationship began.

One day and many treatment rooms later; a second floor was added (along with dozens of new employees who didn't recognize our faithful clients). We realized in time that we had unknowingly swapped some of our best customers to accommodate those who had proven to be more plentiful yet less regular visitors. Our operating costs had risen sharply while our net earnings had actually declined. We were working far harder for only small increases in personal income. Though we prospered in some important ways it just wasn't worth it. I had switched from a happy skincare technician with a wonderful clientele to a stressed out business manager doing heaps of work I did not enjoy. Some great achievement.

Buy the Basics

Perhaps as I have, you'll discover that a minimal collection of skincare devices is quite adequate for performing successful skincare treatments in a thriving practice. You can start with these basic pieces:

- A comfortable non-automatic or semi-automatic facial lounge (one that's easy for you to adjust but also light enough to move for cleaning or other purposes). It should be sturdy and wide enough to accommodate large clients and, ideally, convert to a table for performing back or body treatments.

- 5-diopter magnifying lamp
- Facial steamer or hot towel cabinet, possibly both
- High frequency unit for bacterial control
- Treatment stool that conforms to your height, weight and personal comfort
- Non-abrasive skin brushing/cleansing tool
- Rolling cart or cabinet for product/equipment storage
- 2-place wax heater for face and body purposes (I have the single unit as I do not wax beyond the chin area.)

Pretty much anything else is an option for you to decide upon only after you've run it by the Need, Doubt or Boredom test. Except for backbar and retail products, plus the treatment supplies every esthetician needs, you'll have enough from the above list to competently service almost any client. A microdermabrasion machine is a nice addition to your collection but only if you feel you have the ability to sell that service well. Even then there are other (and perhaps better) methods for exfoliating the skin to achieve a smooth result, such as enzymes or alpha hydroxy acids.

Buying Wisdom

The skincare equipment market today is full of nice-looking, but poorly made junk usually produced overseas. This low quality selection has largely replaced the more competent offerings that once made up most of what was available some years ago.

In 1984 we bought 3 multi-function facial machines for our treatment rooms. After 20 years of faithful service, these machines were still in great operating condition with only minor repairs needed here and there. A more recent unit I bought from another manufacturer proved to be a terrible lesson in shopping for price over materials and workmanship.

Already one of the machine's switches has broken, metal steamer elements rusted and the plastic surround on the magnifying lamp has cracked.

Not only has the seller made it nearly impossible to get the unit serviced, but even if I was given a complete replacement, no doubt I'd have to go through the same trouble sooner or later. I've seen almost new facial lounges break apart under pressure and electrical equipment short out or cords fray and separate from their fittings. This is a shameful waste of money and a huge headache to the esthetician. My advice is to pay a little more (or even a lot more for important items) to get equipment that's domestically (USA) produced or even Canadian made as long as the company has a great reputation and positive customer service history.

Read reviews and ask others on professional blogs about the equipment they use and how it has performed. It's even better to buy high quality used items than poorly built new products at an attractive price. Check around, there's a lot of great gear out there on Craigslist and eBay if you keep your eye out for it. Buy only what you think you'll need, not just equipment or devices you can get for a steal. You may be the one whose money was stolen!

Skincare Products
This is where things tend to get "religious." Every esthetician seems to be a "believer" in one skincare product line or another, each feeling that their line produces the best results for clients. I've heard this battle of the brands go on between estheticians and sales representatives since nearly the first day I entered the profession.

Most of us become indoctrinated in a particular product line as a result of classes and the use of certain products supported by the beauty college we attended. The new esthetician is a very insecure and inexperienced professional, and she or he will often cling to the product line they were trained in because they at least leave school feeling confident in that brand. They may have a few nicely printed certificates of achievement that will look good framed on the treatment room wall, and some will even wear the logo-emblazoned smock gifted to them by the manufacturer. This esthetician has become a true believer, a devoted and convinced convert to the church of Bioestheticoluminessica Plus Forté™.

But, what about all those other professional product lines and the estheticians and clients who are happy with the great results they produce? Aren't those lines just as good? Don't people believe in them, too? Well, yes they do. And why is that? Because those product lines work wonderfully well for their own devoted following, and that includes virtually every product line in the skincare business. It almost doesn't matter what line you choose to work with as long as you're happy with the result it brings, find easy to sell to clients, and is well-supported by the company. Any of them will do.

Still you want to play it smart when it comes to selecting and stocking a treatment line. Here's what the smart professional will do:

- Buy only the products you think you'll need and sell. Not yet sure about what those are yet? Then be very conservative. Start with the minimum order and stick with the basics in the beginning: a couple of cleansers and toners, an exfoliator, some moisturizers (day and evening), eye crème, sunblock and maybe a mask that almost anyone can use for conditioning and hydrating purposes -- perhaps a short acne collection.

- Don't be tempted to carry multiple product lines because you think you might possibly need them. All you'll end up doing is overstocking your shelves and tying up a lot of money needed for other important purposes, such as a little financial backup.

- DO NOT put your product buying decisions in the hands of a sales representative! Those folks know a lot more about writing orders than what your particular practice will need. One Mid-Western day spa I consulted for proudly showed me a plaque awarded by their product vendor for being the #1 customer of their line in the county. Yet, I knew that their retail sales figures (part of the reason they hired me to help) were not exactly something to crow about. That's when I discovered drawers and cabinets crammed full of purchased but unsold skincare products, all faithfully and automatically reordered on schedule by a sales representative who was given the freedom to order for this account!

To be exact, that spa had $119,000 of unsold inventory that had accumulated over several years, much of it aged beyond the expiration date and coming close to bankrupting the owner with debt. It's easy to be a vendor's #1 customer when someone else is writing the wholesale orders even though none of that stock was being sold. By the way, I've known more than one spa in a region that had the same #1 customer distinction from a product company. Petting a professional's ego has long been a proven strategy for milking a few more sales dollars from them, so buyer beware!

- Avoid companies that require high purchase minimum orders if your ability to sell the line is unproven. Enthusiasm can produce an expensive fantasy about customers demanding your products that may not, and probably will not materialize.

- Just because a product company has designed a treatment protocol for you doesn't mean you have to strictly follow it. Many of those facial plans call for layer after layer of product application resulting in more per treatment cost than true improvements on a client's skin. Test the application amounts and methods for yourself and see if you can tell the difference when the application levels are varied. If you can use less, then use less and save your money.

- And remember this: no matter what product line you ultimately settle on and regardless of how much you and your clients love it, you would probably have come to the same place had you selected an entirely different line. Think about it this way: with all of the business and benefits that have come from using the products you currently have, what would you do if that company suddenly went out of business? Would you be forced to just give up and shut down your practice now that your magic products have disappeared? That's not very likely. No doubt you'd find a replacement in a hurry and after a little time adjusting to it you'd probably love the new line as would your customers. You'd be right back on the job and growing your business once more. Keep an open mind and you'll always have an "open" sign!

NOTES / COMMENTS:

1) What discoveries did you make while reading this chapter?

2) How will you use the information you learned?

3) List 3 things you will do to advance your career.

6 How to Have More Career Confidence

Professional confidence is something almost no one can have enough of and, it seems, that most skincare professionals regularly seek to build. Of course, this is especially true when you're newly working with treatment clients. We imagine all sorts of scary things that could go wrong, embarrass us or harm the customer we're treating. Here are some of the most popular "Oh my God, what if THIS happens?" frightful ideas I've heard of (and some I once had myself...):

Newcomer Nightmares

- "What do I say if she asks me how long I've been licensed?"
- "If something goes wrong in a treatment what will I do?"
- "How can I compete for a esthetician position when I have so little job-related experience?"
- "What if she asks me about products I know nothing about?"
- "Clients read everything on the Internet now and might know more about their skin and treatments than I do!"
- "How do I handle a client who has a condition I've never seen or asks about a product I've never heard of?"
- "It's hard for me to market myself or ask for referrals when I'm so new to the profession."

Old-Timer's Tremors

- "If I change my treatments or products my clients will be upset and leave."
- "There's so much new competition and Groupon offers that could ruin my business."
- "If I don't have the newest technology I'll get behind in my practice."
- "All of these doctors hiring estheticians could really reduce my clientele."
- "I should get a CIDESCO certification or become a medical esthetician so I don't get behind."

- "Maybe I should buy that new product line because it's organic, chirally correct, micronized, gluten free, uses wild crafted ingredients, has a patented delivery system or is blessed by fairies, sylphs and water nymphs..."

How many ways are there to make you feel professionally insecure, vulnerable or inadequate? They're only as limited as one's ability to generate such fantasies or whenever you encounter a client who has a knack for sensing weak confidence in someone who is supposed to be a competent and experienced professional. Can you imagine being wheeled into an operating room and asking the surgeon if he or she is skilled in the procedure you're about to have and the response is, "Yeah, I'm pretty sure I am." You do not want to appear this way if building a great service business is your goal.

Some people have successfully performed on stage many, many times and yet experience nervousness before every new audience. Others have prospered in business time and again while an inner voice continually tells them that they're a fraud and a failure. And few people are more insecure about their appearance than accomplished fashion models.

All of these individuals suffer from the same confidence-killing condition—the idea or belief that they can't be or remain good at something they already are or easily could be. But, the fact is that our confidence is dependent more upon what we think in the present moment than what we can do or have done. People who habitually second guess themselves should strive to replace self-limiting ideas with thoughts and expectations that produce a more positive reality. And, for most people who do, it's become a habit.

Seems logical enough, right, but how does one do this? I still have to prove myself in action, don't I? Well, yes, and it was true for me too. But making a goal of building my business among people that came on their own to visit me took much of the performance nervousness away---it distracted me from my fear of relative career inexperience and the idea of acting like a salesperson. Controlling self-defeating thought can do much to shape your confidence and personal success. It's not difficult to do.

Managing Your Thinking to Build Your Confidence

Here's a little technique you can use to help rid yourself of self-doubt or sales fear. It's called "preconceived outcome," which basically means that you imagine exactly what will be the result of something you'll do before you actually do it. You decide in advance how you want something to turn out and then act as if that's what will happen. In my case instead of worrying that a customer will be offended or turned off by my product and service suggestions (fear of personal rejection let's call it) I think of them as being grateful for the help and willing to buy. I ran this picture through my mind, complete with the customer smiling, thanking me and making a purchase or scheduling a future appointment. Now that's an image I could live with!

When I approached my customers with this preconceived outcome in mind, focusing on the client's needs instead of my worrisome inhibitions, products sold easily and clients rebooked. A confident and enthusiastic person has a much easier time winning the approval of another.

How to Overcome Doubt

The famous philosopher Descartes introduced this idea, "I think therefore I am." His idea was to put to rest any doubt about the existence of the self. For our purposes here we'll simply apply this concept to the notion that "We are what we think we are." In other words, if we doubt our own capabilities and skills then that's exactly how we will present ourselves to others.

Here's an example of this: Suppose that you're a fairly new and inexperienced esthetician working in a reputable day spa. You learn that you've been scheduled to perform a facial treatment for Mrs. Jacob Hard-to-Please, a wealthy, extremely selective client who has had facial treatments in all of the top salons and spas from Milan to New York City. She wanted her appointment to be with Monique, a highly skilled Parisian CIDESCO graduate with an impressive French accent.

However, Monique is on holiday with her husband on the Cote D'Azur, so this client must settle for you. Your co-workers have told you that Mrs. Hard-to-Please is a very difficult customer who unnerves everyone because of her demanding attitude and intimidating importance.

So far only Monique has been able to tame her, obviously due to her European accent and education-based confidence. How can you possibly get through this appointment without fear, nervousness and the almost certain risk of being poorly judged?

Easy:

Let's look at some facts before we crumble under the specter of this frightening customer:

- Have you met Mrs. Hard-to-Please yet? No.
- Do you know if she won't like you or appreciate your service? No.
- Is Monique the only person who can truly perform a competent facial for this client? No.
- Is Mrs. Hard-to-Please really the person everyone says she is? Questionable.
- Are you a licensed, skilled and likable professional? Yes.
- Have you ever met so-called difficult people before who ended up liking you? Probably.
- What's the worst thing that can happen to you after your appointment with this client understanding that everyone in the salon knows about her reputation? Not much.
- And, what if she winds up liking you as much or more than Monique? Would you mind that? Of course not; though Monique might!

This is a great opportunity for you at a very small personal and professional risk. If nothing else it's a paid appointment and a chance to learn about people who can only improve your career skills.

So, Here's What You Do:
Clear your mind of any stories about Mrs. Hard-to-Please's personality or background.

Think of her for who she truly is—a human being interested in looking and feeling better, needing a skilled professional to help her do that. And that person, of course, is you.

Imagine Mrs. Hard-to-Please as Mrs. Easy-to-Please, someone who is open and willing to have a great facial appointment with a warm and caring professional—also you!

Now, plan your experience with Mrs. Easy-to-Please: you're looking forward to meeting this fascinating world traveler, learning about her needs and giving her a great treatment that matches or exceeds her expectations.

You'll greet this client with a smile, enthusiasm and the knowledge that you have the skill to perform a wonderfully satisfying facial treatment for her.

In your mind visualize Mrs. Easy-to-Please as relaxed, friendly and happy to meet someone new in the salon, someone who might offer her an even superior treatment than the ones she's had in the past. You can do this, too!

Know that you're going to take the time to fully interview this client explaining that you want to be sure you plan the exact right treatment for her needs and expectations. Listen, write down what she says in front of her, and then tell her what you plan to do during that treatment, and why.

Be sure to ask enough questions about her skin, past treatments and facial preferences so she feels you care about her and are an exceptional and thorough skincare professional.

Assume that you know exactly what to do and then go about the treatment as you feel it would be best for her. Then notice how little time and attention you spent worrying about working with this customer. In the end she'll love your work and may even reschedule with you instead of Monique!

This is exactly how to overcome fear and doubt in any situation no matter how worried you may feel beforehand. Those unhappy emotions are attached to ideas that have nothing to do with the approaching appointment. By changing your unpleasant thoughts about something you also change the feelings those thoughts conjure up and, therefore, banish the nervous anticipation.

Doubt and worry are habits of the mind. They are old and ritualistic routines that make you imagine the worst of outcomes in situations that have not yet happened. Memories of the past are only that, not a firm reason that some new encounter will reproduce the negative experience you've had before. Think of anything that once frightened you the first time you tried to do it but no longer does – riding a bicycle, driving a car, skiing down a steep hill. Can you see how little by little the fear was replaced by confidence, skill, and eventually great comfort? All it took to get you there was the determination to learn and a passionate desire to master something you really wanted to do.

Your skincare career is like that too -- in time, with patience and belief in yourself, you'll become as competent as anyone in the profession. The main thing is not to shrink away from challenge but to embrace growth as both an opportunity and a game you want to win at. If you do that every time you confront something that intimidates you, you'll be one step closer to having a great career in esthetics!

<u>NOTES / COMMENTS:</u>

1) What discoveries did you make while reading this chapter?

2) How will you use the information you learned?

3) List 3 things you will do to advance your career.

7 How to Earn More Money in Each Appointment

There's no secret to building your service and sales ticket with clients, but there are methods that work better than others if you use them skillfully and routinely. To do this you should begin by having a thorough working knowledge of what's available to you for making money. As obvious as this sounds, few skin professionals ever stop to consider just how rich their opportunity to build income actually is. Let's start with a simple list:

Services:
- Facial treatments
- Anti-aging treatments (microdermabrasion, peels, etc.)
- Waxing
- Lash extensions
- Hand treatments
- Body treatments
- Makeup application
- And whatever else you happen to offer where you work

Retail products:
- All skincare products
- Makeup and cosmetic brushes
- Body products
- Spa accessories
- Cleansing tools, etc.

Wow! There's a lot of opportunity to increase sales in your profession, isn't there? And looking at the above retail list how many of those products do you feel your average client might find appealing for her or his interest in personal care? I'll bet you have something for everyone. The question is, how do you make the most of every client visit for growing your income while also enhancing your client's service satisfaction? It's easy if you work with a simple plan and learn to overcome some very expensive and incorrect ideas that may be holding back your true potential.

Before we talk about selling more services and retail products let's first look at the idea of sales as something you should master. When you think of yourself as having to be a salesperson what are the ideas, images and feelings that come to mind? Do you feel nervous or uncomfortable? Is your image of a salesperson someone who is pushy and aggressive, possibly insincere and pressuring? Are you worried about negative reactions from clients for suggesting additional services or new retail items?

Maybe you've had an unpleasant response from a customer in the past that you don't want to experience again. You may have convinced yourself that selling is an unprofessional way to conduct your skincare career. Any of these ideas could prevent you from growing your business with clients. I want to help free you from such barriers to a better income and future.

When I first began my skincare practice I was literally terrified to ask a client to reschedule with me. My fear of rejection was so severe that I could barely get the words, "Did you want to reschedule your appointment?" up through my tightly closed throat. I'm sure I sounded like a squeaking mouse and was probably unknowingly shaking my head "no" while forcing out the frightful question.

Of course, no one did reschedule with me, and because of this I was depressed, dejected, and certain that I didn't have what it took to succeed as a career esthetician. I imagined: maybe it was because I was a man. Maybe I was lousy at performing facial treatments. What if I had body odor or bad breath and didn't know it? Or maybe I was just too timid to persuade clients to see me again.

Whatever it was, my clientele wasn't building and that fact could lead to career failure. I was miserable and going broke.

Once I learned about what sales and selling actually was, I could stop being afraid of suggesting to my clients the products and services they wanted or needed. I won't exhaust you with a repeat of the tired, "You're not selling, you're helping!" mantra. If you feel like you're selling but don't feel good about it then no philosophical statement will do much to change that.

We've all suffered the person who when seeing our less-than-giddy facial expression orders us to SMILE! I don't know about you but few things on earth make me want to smile less than being told to. There's nothing like an unsolicited critique about one's expression to transform "the look" into something even more sour. So, trying to sweeten up your reflexive distaste for selling with a nice philosophy just won't get very far. Let me offer a more realistic approach to building your business income through opportunities found in service and retail sales.

What is "Selling?"
Passing a shoe store window at the mall, you see a gorgeous pair of heels on a pedestal surrounded by party decor and a photograph of a beautiful woman embraced by a handsome chiseled man. You stop to look; the fantasy and feelings stimulated by the display images rapidly run through your mind, all connected to those sexy shoes. Maybe you even want to go in and try them on. That's "selling."

Before leaving for work you probably shower, style your hair, possibly apply makeup and choose an attractive or professional outfit to wear. Why do you go through this time-consuming ritual every day? Because you want to impress your clients and win them back again, of course. That's also "selling." Whether we're readying for work, using a more pleasant tone in our voice when talking to someone we're attracted to, or dressing up for an important job interview we do so with the goal in mind to gain something favorable for us. That is also "selling."

What's important to understand is that the act of selling is not, in fact, sales. We can't make someone like us, no matter how well we groom. Likewise, we can't make anyone buy something they don't want even if that's our intention which, of course, it wouldn't be. All we can do is to prepare an appearance or environment that makes a sale more likely to happen.

Expensive and Incorrect Assumptions About Clients

Where did so many professionals acquire the magical power of knowing how much money a client is willing to spend while visiting the salon? Is their car rusty and needing a push to start after their appointment? Do they come in dressed in rags or try to trade homemade jam for a facial? Arc they counting pennies out of a jar to pay for their body waxing? Even if they've recently lost their job do you really know what they do with their money however much they may still have (which you also don't know)?

When we assume that a client has reached some mysterious resistance point about a service or retail ticket then we're claiming an ability to read minds, see through the leather sides of wallets and telepathically view the balance of people's bank accounts. That's a truly remarkable feat, except that you can't do it, nor should you try to.

We have no idea what a customer is open to spending, we can only test their potential desire for the services we offer and products we sell. But, if we allow our fears or beliefs to act as facts then we'll automatically and consistently put costly limits on our business and income. Is it really worth it just to avoid a possible mild "no, thank you" from a nice customer? That can easily add up to thousands of dollars in willfully refused service and retail sales. Can you afford it?

The truth is that people love to buy things that make them feel good. The salon is "an emporium of feel good" indulgences, facial treatments in particular, unless you've mastered the art of turning bliss into misery. Americans are consumption-happy citizens brought up in a culture of materialism and endless desires. While I'm not in business to take advantage of consumer-driven people I am also unlikely to thrive if I attempt to curb their habits. Successful selling is easy if you know how to blend positive emotions into the right "buying" setting. All you have to do is to keep the salon environment filled with fun and enthusiasm. Downers do not sell.

I once was attracted to a roll of wallpaper high out of reach among others in a decorating shop. The paper looked intriguing and I had been searching for something special to use in a bathroom at home. When I asked a sales clerk to bring the paper roll down so I could take a closer look he informed me matter-of-factly, "Well, it's VERY expensive!" Annoyed, I asked him if I had given him the impression that price was a factor. "No," he responded defensively. "I just thought you should know."

I wasn't sure if the salesperson assumed that I couldn't afford the paper or if he was just hoping to avoid shocking me with the price tag (which turned out to be high only in his world, not mine). In any case he certainly wasn't eager to go to the trouble of retrieving that wallpaper for me.

While I did want the paper, I didn't want to buy it from him so I passed on it. That was quite a loss for his employer.

Closing a Sale

Few things make an esthetician more uncomfortable than being charged with having to "close a sale" with a customer whether they're selling services, service upgrades or a skincare regimen.

You may just hate the idea. This reaction arises because of those awful images and negative feelings that run through your mind and body as you see yourself pressuring an innocent customer

into buying something she doesn't really need or can't afford. You're being a terrible, insensitive and greedy person if you do something like that (or so you might think).

So there goes your client out of the salon with a bag of products she shouldn't have purchased which will now cause her to pay her rent late or even deny the kids their dinner, and all because of money-hungry YOU! So, of course, you're not going to do it no matter how much your boss tells you that it's part of your job. Your ethics just won't allow you to.

It's important to know how sales actually happen and how you can do well with them free of guilt or fear. Here's how a sale happens in your business:

A client willingly visits the salon for your services, which means that she values them. You have no idea how much she will spend or how much money she has to spend unless you ask her, and you're certainly not going to do that. Whether it's a product or a treatment you're describing to her, you present it in a way that makes it seem appealing, fun, beneficial or almost magical. An example: "Diane, your hands are pretty dry and we could make them feel like silk if we do a paraffin softening treatment during your facial. It feels heavenly!" You did not ask, "Did you want to get or buy" the service in question.

All you did was describe it appealingly. A sale happens when clients decide in their own minds that what you spoke about sounds like something they want. You don't close a sale, the client does. You simply dressed up the idea and won an agreement to purchase. That's it, over.

Have you ever spoken rudely to or scolded a store clerk when you bought something on impulse? Probably not. Imagine when placing that purse or pair of earrings on the sales counter you decide to blame the person ringing up the sale as being responsible for your sudden, unnecessary expense, "You know, I'm going to buy this bag I don't need but I want to say that I think it's really unethical of you to put it on display so I'd be forced to have it!" I doubt that's going to happen.

We accept our role in the buy. And what if the clerk tried to talk you out of purchasing the bag because he didn't think you should be spending your money that way? Would you be happy with him about that?

The point is that you can't close a sale, so abandon that idea right here. But, you can inspire someone to buy something just through a simple and enthusiastic description. When I landed my first job in cosmetic sales at a small makeup boutique I knew practically nothing about the products it sold.

I had no clue about how to sell a foundation, mascara or eye shadow. Having to sell those products terrified me, especially since the boutique owner watched the employees throughout the day, counting their sales results hour by hour. I felt constantly on the edge of employment doom, any minute expecting to be escorted out the door after a dismal day of receipts.

That was hardly an inspiring way to work in a sales job. What I learned to do (and what worked very well) was instead of talking to customers about what they might need was to talk about products I thought were pretty cool. New lipstick colors and beautiful eye shadow shades made me want to see them on the people who shopped at the store. So, I'd simply say, "Hi! You know we just got these new makeup colors in and I'd love to see how they look on you. Would you mind if I try a couple of them on your eyes and lips?"

Women rarely refused a chance to see something that might make them look better, so most sat right down and allowed me to apply away. Of course, if I liked the effect I'd play it up: "Wow, look how that plum shade makes the green in your eyes pop. It's amazing! And that deep coral lip color is a very complementary shade on you."

I never had to ask the customer if they wanted to buy the makeup, in most cases they just bought it. Even though I was selling, it was the customer who made the sale happen, not me. There was nothing to be afraid of. This is quite different (and certainly feels better!) than being ordered to tell a customer, usually in a bland, flat voice, about a special item at checkout: "Um, this week we're offering our makeup spritzer for only $15.99. Did you want to get one?" Nothing said about what it can do, how it can make the customer look, or even any true connection between that product and the seller except for a supervisor listening to see if they're following protocol.

We've all experienced this and most of us have probably passed on the pitch. But how about this approach, "By the way, before you go we have the coolest finishing spray for foundation that makes the skin glow like satin! Just a couple of quick sprays after you apply your makeup and you'll look dewey and fresh the whole day! I love this product and use it myself, and it's only $15.99 this week." No need to ask if the customer wants to buy it, just let her decide in her own mind. You can talk about something that could make your customer look better while avoiding that "salesy" feeling you don't like.

So, begin building your income by finding products or services you really like and then rehearse how to describe them in a way that makes them sound truly appealing. Remember, you're not trying to push someone to buy the things you describe, just sharing your very positive feelings about them with the possibility that your customer will agree.

It should make no difference to you at all whether the customer buys on your story or not, that will only cause you to feel inauthentic and unnatural. Just have fun talking about what you like so that others have something to like too, and possibly take home. There are statistics showing that the more customers spend in a business the more satisfied they are. Would you want to deny someone that extra satisfaction? Spread the joy and earn a better living at the same time!

How to Sell Products and Services

Okay, exhale and just relax a little. I know you may dislike this sales business but inspiring customers to spend a little extra money with you doesn't have to be scary or uncomfortable. In fact, you can even make a sort of game of it. I enjoyed doing that because it turned the act of selling into something more stimulating to me: learning and growing.

Having virtually no business in my beginning year of professional esthetics and lots of time to think about that lack of customers I decided to set a goal---I would turn every customer I received into three or more. The idea was simple: whenever new clients came in for a particular service I would attempt to convince them to try at least two other services I performed or products I sold, thus, turning each client into two more.

Here's how it went:
- New facial client: suggest facial waxing and retail products
- New waxing client: suggest facial services and retail products
- New product customer: suggest facial treatments and waxing

Rather than needing to find three new clients I could make three clients out of one. That meant I could make more money from fewer customers.

Simple Selling Techniques Anyone Can Do

The Wax Pot of Gold

Before my schedule blossomed full of higher-end facial treatments I used to love stand-alone eyebrow or facial waxing appointments with new customers. Talk about a golden opportunity to sell your higher ticket services! There I had a fresh new face lying right in the sweet spot for promoting facial services, and I never missed the chance to offer those. Try this simple script with a new waxing client:

"I am wondering if you ever receive facial treatments?" (Doesn't matter if the answer is yes or no) "Since you're here would you mind if I take a close look at your skin and tell you what I see happening with it?" No one ever declined me the option to do that. There under the magnifying lamp I see the dry, flaking skin, the fine lines, clogged follicles and everything else we work to correct in our services. "Your skin is a little dehydrated and has dulled because of a thick dead skin buildup. I could easily give it a refined look and a glow that'll make you look years younger!"

While your suggestion won't convince everyone to sign up for a treatment, it will win many of them, and that's all I'm hoping for;

never worrying about those who may decline the idea. Just move right along if you don't get the booking you wanted. There's no point in wasting time wondering what went wrong or why the client passed on the offer. All you'll do is push your confidence off balance, and there's nothing useful in that.

Bye-bye, and Then Buy

Whenever scheduling a new facial customer, whether it's you or someone else at the appointment calendar, always request that this new person bring in all of his or her current skincare products so you can evaluate them. For acne clients it's useful to check out their hair products, too. I can't recall a single time when someone declined to do that though they will sometimes forget (you can always remind when confirming the appointment). I love this part of a new client session (always allow an extra 10-15 minutes for it), as it's a fascinating and valuable learning experience for both client and esthetician.

As I pull item after item out of the new customer's bag, I see a larger picture of her or his purchasing and use habits... everything from a small collection of the cheapest grocery store products to high-end or professional brands that cost far more money. This is a perfect opportunity to accomplish 3-important things:

- To learn what your clients' personal care culture is like and what has been affecting their skin.
- To evaluate what they need as opposed to what they already use.
- To sell new skincare products and possibly upgrade a service.

You'll have to trust me on this one but when clients go to the trouble to bring in their bag of products they're almost always ready to replace them or at least try something new. The mere fact they may have many skincare items in their collection is a strong clue that they enjoy using them. New possibilities can be exciting and desirable!

Now, if your only goal here is to make a big sale then your purpose may be questionable. Not every customer has purchased products from me just because I suggested them, but most of them have and still do. It's the majority customer-type that you'll want to be concerned with and not so much the occasional "thanks but no thanks" visitor. These are the customers who value their skin's appearance and your expert advice more than most, and they're ready to do whatever it takes to look and feel better.

When you evaluate your clients' products assure them that they've been doing the right thing by caring for their skin but then ask if they would be open to a few recommendations from your professional lines to improve their home care approach. Make a note of your suggested replacements to review with them following their facial.

I usually begin with a few items that will make the biggest difference in the skin and then work back to the staples (cleanser and toner) during a later visit. Many customers will buy everything you suggest right then and there but I like to develop the product relationship over time. This simple technique is worth thousands of dollars in sales every year.

New Season, New Reason (to buy products and services!)
Estheticians often ask me how they can sell additional products to clients who have already purchased a complete skincare regimen from them. I love this question because the answer is, "It's really easy to do!" First of all you need to consider the customer in question. Anyone willing to plunk down the funds to purchase a full skincare regimen is a person willing to do it again and who has the financial means to.

This is a customer who clearly enjoys purchasing and using personal care products. And, as we've discussed before, we won't decide for ourselves whether or not we've arrived at this customer's spending limit, will we? Of course not! We'll merely help these clients do what they like (with more benefits to them than an expensive bottle of wine or a weekend under resort sun).

The best way to use this selling method is by preparing your client to expect it in advance, without calling it a selling point, of course. Here's what I tell my skincare clients during their very first treatment:

> *"From time to time, especially just before a major seasonal change such as summer to fall and winter to spring, I'll want to adjust your facial treatments and home care routine to address the effects of harsh weather on your skin."*

That's a reasonable request, isn't it? It's also the correct way to keep your treatment programs working at their optimal level. I ask every regular facial client I reschedule between August 15th and September 15th or between March 15th and April 15th to bring in their current regimen for review during the next treatment. I allow a few extra minutes for this brief session. Then, if I determine that we need a new or different sunblock, heavier moisturizer for the coming winter, conditioning mask for severely dry weather or any other essential product for the approaching season I can suggest it at that time.

You'll also want to offer seasonally upgraded treatments that address the negative skin influences changing weather can produce. Super hydrating facial masks during the arid winter months and special ones rich in anti-oxidants for times when people are much more exposed to outdoor elements, such as summer are perfect suggestions. An extra $15.00 or so on the service charge may not seem like much when paired with the age-protection or younger appearance of moisture rich skin results your treatment offers. Remember, your customers see you to look and feel better; exactly what we achieve in our skilled services. If you hold back, your clients lose the opportunity to experience an improved result while you forfeit the income.

That Little in-Between Facial Treatment

When clients who you haven't seen for a longer than usual cycle suddenly return to your appointment schedule, you can often catch up a little by suggesting a second facial treatment in two weeks instead of waiting the typical four. There are numerous skin conditions that could be remedied by a closer second treatment visit. In such cases I often suggest these:

- A deeper skin peel and rehydration treatment to correct dull, tired-looking skin
- An additional extraction-focused facial to get all of the skin impactions that built up during their absence

While not every client will opt to have this faster repeat visit, many will, and any additional appointments are opportunities to build your income. Words are valuable influencers: they cost you nothing so use them liberally!

A Word About Makeup Services and Sales

It seems that it's the rare esthetician who performs makeup services and sells makeup products. The usual explanation for this has to do with not feeling confident about makeup design or making correct color choices for customers. And since this short segment is for those who feel similarly, I will assume that you could use a little help making money from this golden but often overlooked opportunity.

Understanding the Average Makeup Customer

You may think that successfully working with and making money from makeup requires great design skills, skills you may not believe you have or are even willing to train for. Erase those ideas as they will limit your career and deny you some very easy income. Visit any department store makeup counter and what you'll observe is that most customer/salesperson interaction involves advice and information but not direct makeup application. In fact, a makeup artist's highly developed design abilities may actually work against the wishes of the average makeup shopper, which is to pick out a few new colors or learn about how to better apply one or two common products.

In my early years of makeup work I signed on as a freelance artist with a San Francisco talent agency. They contracted with the major cosmetic companies to supply makeup designers for special promotions, usually held in large upscale retail stores. Our job was to learn the current design campaign and push it on customers who scheduled for a complimentary application. All too often these promotions featured some nightmarish fantasy concocted by a New York director who seemed to have never met a real makeup customer.

Here would be a conservative soccer mom sitting in my makeup stool, unknowingly about to be transformed into a kabuki actor. While the other artists did their duty and painted on those awful faces (frequently resulting in the victim running straight to the restroom to erase it), I merely asked my clients what they had questions about regarding our colors and/or application techniques. Their requests were always so simple: What was a good way to shape the eyebrows? What eye shadows were right for them? How could they find the right foundation match? Which lipstick shades looked best for their eyes and hair color?

All they wanted was easy-to-offer advice that almost anyone with even a modest interest in makeup could learn to provide. I don't recall a single time when a customer requested a complete day-to-night makeover or certainly nothing close to the look we were promoting. As much as some of my employers were annoyed by my refusal to follow their plan (and forever tried to force me to do it), they wouldn't fire me because my product sales results usually exceeded that of all the other artists combined. Money does talk.

The same concept is true at my makeup bar today. While there are clients for high-fashion makeup applications, most women are looking for a simple but attractive approach for applying daily use.

I'm by no means a great makeup artist. In fact, I've never called the way I apply makeup "art" at all, instead and more accurately… I'm a makeup designer. The average woman is not looking for "artistry" when it comes to doing her own makeup, just a look that's simple, natural and easy to apply.

If you have even modest skills in selecting color or advising on routine products such as properly applying mascara or eyebrow shaping you can earn extra income just by including this important beauty department in your business. For those who are serious about growing a skincare practice and earnings, consider these makeup related advantages:

Often you'll not need to perform a full makeup design in order to work with and sell cosmetics to your customers. Simple application tips and color ideas will generally cover it. Remember, this is all about removing obstacles to growing your career not about having to master something that isn't at the heart of your practice goals. And as I wrote earlier, the more relationships you have with your customers the more they will spend in your salon. Why give your business away to the Shiseido or Lancome counter? Always strive to be as valuable to your clients as possible.

NOTES / COMMENTS:

1) What discoveries did you make while reading this chapter?

2) How will you use the information you learned?

3) List 3 things you will do to advance your career.

8 Career Killers: How to Ruin Your Chances of Succeeding

Why would anyone want to sabotage something they seem to have wanted so much and invested a great deal of time and money in? Sadly, I have seen this act performed countless times over the years by legions of estheticians, including some of those formerly under my own employment. It's like watching a budding future in professional skincare willfully neglected to wilt and die like an unwanted houseplant. To witness such career self-destruction defies the imagination, yet it's an astonishingly common occurrence. What causes a potentially or presently successful esthetician to suddenly fly off the rails?

Why Many Careers Fail Before They Really Get Started

Sometimes skincare professionals lose interest in the work they thought they would spend a lifetime doing. Somehow it failed to hold their attention, so off they went to try something else. Occasionally, one finds the career too physically demanding, financially disappointing or requiring more time and patience than they could give. Then there are those who seem to have difficulty holding onto a job, any job, for very long.

Finding yourself licensed to perform skincare in a small town with few interested customers or those with the means to afford esthetic   services will certainly make a skincare career challenging to survive in. Any number of things can make someone lose heart and walk away from a profession once fueled by a great deal of desire.

The truth is that the majority of estheticians who remain working in the profession wind up struggling for years on a career that seems to never get very far and even declines over time.

There are plenty reasons for this outcome, ones that can easily be avoided when you understand the business you're in and follow a sensible plan for success.

How to Slowly Starve a Career to Death

Careers, like children, need time, patience and nurturing in order to learn, grow and thrive into maturity. Remove or inadequately provide these life-building basics and the result can be disastrous. Just hoping for the best to happen, whatever that best means, will not get the job done. In spite of the popular notion that focused dreaming will eventually produce your greatest desires, most people will discover that real work and discipline are the main ingredients in achievement.

Unfortunately, many estheticians find these personal qualities lackingonce the pre-planned course of beauty school is behind them. These newly minted professionals are left to work out the necessary tasks of businessbuilding on their own. This can lead to a frustrating and unsuccessful set of experiences if not skillfully attended to. And while it's a potential advantage to have the resources of an experienced business coach or partner, the best assistance will come from someone who has thorough knowledge in the esthetics, spa or beauty industry.

To help you understand how to avoid sabotaging your own career future I've listed some of the main mistakes esthetics (and other) professionals make that can delay or ruin any chance for achieving a satisfying future in skincare.

Preston's "Toxic Ten"

1. **Delaying Entry into the Esthetics Field**
   Here someone receives an esthetics license but waits indefinitely before seeking a job in the profession. This delay may cause the loss of precious time that could have been devoted to getting an esthetics business organized, established in the community and attracting a comfortable client base.

2. **Frequently Changing Workplaces**
   Anytime you uproot a plant you cause a condition called "root shock" which, hopefully, only leads to temporary wilting and a pause in the growing process. Every time an esthetician changes jobs her or his progress timetable will be set back a full year, and that is only if one remains close to their existing customers. If you move farther away where you have to start from scratch the setback will be even longer.

3. **Limiting Working Days and Hours**
   I've met few estheticians willing to work a 40-hour week and even fewer open to stretching those hours to capture new customers or accommodate current ones. Sure, there are realities to consider such as children and even a second job but many of these professionals simply prefer a fixed and minimal schedule. That sort of rigidity will not only deny potential new client opportunities, but may also fail

to satisfy an employer who needs a more flexible and ambitious esthetician on the team.

4. **Declining to Perform Certain Types of Esthetic Service Work**

Dislike Brazilian bikini waxing? Disinterested in makeup services? Grossed out by blackhead extractions? That's all fine, but remember this: the average esthetician has an appointment schedule where facial or body waxing represents up to 60% of any given day. And, while makeup services may not be the most popular ones in the salon, they do offer the opportunity to meet potential new facial and retail customers. Also note that blackhead extraction is one of the most client-valued results of all skincare treatments. To turn away these or any other service functions is to severely limit your career growth or usefulness to an employer.

5. **Refusing to Sell or Improve Sales in Retail Products**

By now you've probably heard this many times but, because of its huge importance, I'll repeat it: the selling of retail products will have a big impact not only on your sales commission income but also on your client retention. Let these sales get away and your clients will be all the more available for competitors to attract them away from you. And, product help is a basic client assistance obligation for the responsible skincare professional.

6. **Frequent Absenteeism, the Need for Numerous Days Off for Personal Reasons, Moving or Cancelling Client Appointments, and Leaving the Salon when Nothing is on the Schedule**

Treat your career like an option or nuisance in your daily life and watch how quickly it will either sit frozen or fade away. Days spent away from your practice are expensive in terms of lost income, lost opportunity to receive call-in business. They are also an annoyance to both clients and employers alike. Some estheticians have a penchant for asking for weekend days off or needing to attend special events such as weddings and family gatherings or vacations. Others can't bear to wait out the boring, unfilled hours experienced by anyone building a new skincare practice. For those who will struggle with these facts of work life esthetics may not be the ideal career for you.

7. **Product Line Worship**
Sure you love the products you were trained to use and are experienced in. Yes, your clients were happy with them and they built a nice retail business for you. But, when you choose to work for a new salon you may be required to learn and use an entirely different product brand than the one you're used to. This can be a very tough adjustment for many routine-oriented estheticians. Some will attempt to reject the new products or push the salon owner into switching lines just to escape change. I've seen salon after salon with shelves stocked by bits and pieces of various skincare brands, all requested by estheticians who demanded them, promising to support and sell those products yet only to quit and abandon the inventory to a sorry employer. Wise esthetician will care more about service quality than the particular products they use in those services, knowing that all professional brands deliver pretty much the same results with customers, regardless of a company's philosophy or patents. An open mind is an open door to business success.

8. **Complaining, Complaining and Complaining**
There are people who can't see anything but the downside of life. These are the "glass half empty" professionals who accept a job only to find everything wrong with it, clients, coworkers and life in general from day one. Nothing is good enough, management isn't fair, teammates are unfriendly and competitive, the customers are rude — on

And on it goes. They don't like the work schedule, have a low opinion of the salon facilities and equipment, feel that they know more about their profession than anyone else and have a litany of excuses for their short-comings. We've probably all encountered one of them. These folks may be better suited for a government job than one in the hospitality or beauty industry.

9. **Turning one's Personal Drama into the Client's Experience**

Back when I was a spa employer I was aware that one of my estheticians was having serious relationship difficulties. But it was only when a loyal client told me that this particular professional cried throughout the entire facial while telling her sad tale did I learn just how poor my employee's judgment was. So, that resulted in a free client facial, an apology from me, and a corrective action meeting. I've also witnessed salon owners openly sharing money worries with customers and employees, hardly the kind of thing that builds customer confidence and a sense of well-being in a workplace. Esthetics is part beauty business and part entertainment business, that is, we create both visual changes on the skin while helping to soothe and calm our customers. Anything that deviates from that is simply out of the question, yet the drift into unprofessional behavior and conversation is too tempting for some estheticians to resist. Paid service time belongs to the client and, even when it is they who initiate delicate personal subjects, the smart professional will listen but lead the client to a better focus.

10. **Undercharging for Services and Devoting Excessive Time to Them**

This is an expensive tendency of the guilt-ridden and price-fearing skincare professional. Secretly believing that his or her services aren't worth the money their salon or private practice charges for them, this nervous esthetician will undercut the price, fail to charge for add-ons such as mask upgrades or waxing, or spend far too long in the performance of a treatment. But, not only does this practice limit one's income but also reinforces to both the professional and the customer that where confidence is missing, prices can be manipulated -- usually in a downward direction.

NOTES / COMMENTS:

1) What discoveries did you make while reading this chapter?

2) How will you use the information you learned?

3) List 3 things you will do to advance your career.

9 How to Stay Motivated & Happy

The world is full of books, CD's, articles and speakers who talk about how to be motivated and happy. They'll tell you that happiness is a choice and that you can be content "right this minute" if you want to be. Others will point out that lasting motivation depends on setting meaningful goals and pursuing them or having passion for certain things you want, or starting your day with an affirming mantra.

All of them are right. The trouble is that you can read, listen to or try any of these methods and still end up discouraged about your chances for career success or your credibility in the profession. You might even wonder if any of those empowering words and practices are as helpful as promised.

Well, here's one more piece of advice for you: whatever it is you are feeling and thinking simply acknowledge and accept it, and then keep going about your day in spite of it. Yes, I'm suggesting that you go ahead and suffer, indulge in those critical thoughts, and wallow in self-doubt and worry. Don't try to get rid it. Don't attempt to run away from it. And whatever you do, don't pretend that you've somehow magically been transformed because you've heard some encouraging words that temporarily raised you from your malaise.

I don't want you to run over a path of hot coals. What I'm asking you to do is to stand still, barefooted, so that you feel the full searing pain of them. Why? Because I want you to get sick and tired of self-punishment as soon as possible. The best way to stop feeling like that is to expose yourself to it as much as you possibly can. Stand there and suffer until you have no desire to do that anymore. Only then you will be open to trying something different. You'll welcome almost any alternative to spending another day in misery and self-pity.

The truth is, people change and grow at exactly the moment they're ready to. That time often arrives after an extended period of joyless frustration or fruitless attempts to avoid something unpleasant. And when that time comes, you might want to begin focusing on some or all of the following:

What's Gone Right In Your Career Since You Began It?
- Do you have more clients than last year?
- Have your professional skills increased?
- Do you know more helpful people than you used to?
- Have you received compliments about your work lately?

Think about everything that is going right for you instead of what you feel is not. If you find that you have gained more than lost, then you are making normal, positive progress. There's no need to push harder or wonder how things might have been if you had done something differently. Look at what you actually have, not what you think you don't or believe you should.

What Makes You Feel Great About Your Work?
- What's happening inside when people tell you how wonderful your treatments are or how much they appreciate you?
- Are you happy to see your acne clients improve?
- When performing a facial massage does it please you to hear how much your client enjoys it?
- Are your spirits lifted when a satisfied customer tells you that she'll recommend you to everyone she knows?
- Isn't it wonderful that you're not working in a bank, in an office cubicle, or the municipal court?
- Don't you love the cash clients slip to you for a job well done?
- Now, what would you rather think about and feel while reflecting on your career?

Consider What a Remarkably Positive Job You Have

It's truly amazing, isn't it? All day long we see customers who are happy to see us and love the way we make them look and feel. How many careers offer anything as sweet as that? Dentistry? Tax preparation? Insurance sales? Not likely. We have a marvelous profession that some among us have worked hard to turn into a career stocked with problems. Why would anyone want to do that?

Let It Come and Let It Go

When you catch yourself worrying about business, your negative boss or the clients who haven't come back, become aware of the track you're on and stop yourself if you can. Search for a thought that makes you feel better and then think about it only, like switching from a depressing song to an uplifting one. Thoughts are merely ideas that can produce feelings either good or bad. The good news is that we can change them as quickly as we want to. I'm not suggesting that you simply ignore something of any real importance. But unpleasant things you continually work over in your mind will never get better.

What you get by thinking about bad feelings is even more of them and a loss of energy. This converts into a negative, self-defeating outlook that extends out into your future, a time that hasn't even happened. Yet, you're already feeling bad about it. Disengaging from the routine of negative thinking becomes a habit in itself over time, one you'll be glad to keep!

Visit Your Professional Facebook Page and Post Something Positive

Don't have a Facebook page? Then get one! It's free and you can use it to keep in touch with current customers and potentially meet new ones. Require yourself to think about and write on positive, funny or heart-warming subjects others will want to read. What inspires others will inspire you, too.

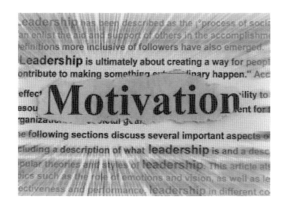

Maintaining a Facebook page is one way to demand the best of yourself daily. It can develop into wonderfully a healthy discipline. However... you may have seen estheticians who post personal complaints about customers in some of the professional groups, griping about no-shows and poor tippers, or people with stupid, unrealistic expectations. What an unfortunate way to portray a career not to mention how that affects every skincare professional's image.

Keep Inspiring Reading Material in Your Treatment Room and Read it as Often as Possible

Uh oh, a last second cancellation has just blown your mood into the street and was run over by a semi-truck of resentment. You aren't happy about it, not one little bit. And this was the client you agreed to stay late for when you had a hundred important things you mighthave done instead. How could she do this to you? Such a rude, ungrateful, thoughtless...

Stop right now! Just stop. Sit down, take a deep breath, relax, and let the focus on this seemingly great injustice pass. Just let it work its way through your tense body and mind. Soon it will roll to a standstill you'll suddenly discover a little clear space where you can think of something better, a more enlightening idea to illuminate the black void.

Now, open one of your inspirational books and begin to read. It doesn't matter what chapter or page you start with—if the subject is teaching you how to see the events of life in a more constructive light then virtually any example will be useful to you at this moment. Better yet, if your book has a chapter on dealing with life's little upsets then thumb right to it and study awhile.

Almost immediately you'll discover that your flaming dance with disgust will soothe into a deeper kind of knowing that this momentary and frankly rare annoyance wasn't such a big deal after all. In fact, look how it helped you to finally open that inspiring book you've been meaning to read which now has you feeling good about your career again.

Think About the Possibilities Ahead

You may be content with exactly where your practice is right now: full of happy clients and unburdened by business ownership stress. If that's the case then you're home free, though you may still have those irritating moments of frustration all working people occasionally experience.

If you are the type of person who loves to look beyond the present and think about what more you can do as an professional esthetician, you might want to turn your low moods and outlook toward creating new career goals that could distract you from doubt and dismay.

This leads us back to knowing who we are or want to be as a skincare professional. Not only that, consider what will you be able to do when your income doubles as it most certainly will if you put your time and heart into your work. Think about it:

- If you're saving your cash tips instead of quickly spending them as many people do, you can plan a nice vacation to somewhere you love. Goals do have a way of enforcing spending discipline. So, where do you want to go?

111

- Won't it be nice to upgrade your esthetics equipment, redecorate your treatment room or take an extra personal day off because you can afford to?
- Still can't afford to join your friends at that exciting skincare show just yet? Staying positive and focused will enable you to make your travel reservations with everyone else.
- Is your vision to open your own esthetics studio someday? The sooner you refocus your attention on what's working well in your career the sooner you will see your dream become a reality.

And consider some of the following future-enhancing actions:

Try Writing a Public Presentation Outline On Skincare That You Would Give at a Client's Home or in a Classroom Setting

Don't worry about how good you think it is or whether you could comfortably deliver the presentation. Just require yourself to do something new and outside of your comfort level. No one ever needs to see it but you, yet the exercise will help to improve your writing skills and organize a message you'd like others to hear, clients or professionals. Who knows? It just might lead to a speakership or a trade magazine article. Challenge yourself!

Work On Your Customer Service

Do you believe you're doing the best you possibly can when it comes to making clients feel comfortable and appreciated? Are you calling your new customers a day or two after their treatment to learn how they feel about the results? Do you tell your clients each and every appointment how much you value them? This isn't about giving away service add-ons or offering unexpected discounts to customers. I'm referring to simple verbal gestures of individual care that clients love to hear. These cost nothing but a tiny amount of time. And the best part: they will make you feel great, too!

Experience a Facial (yes, you!)

As incredible as it seems estheticians don't receive facial treatments nearly often enough themselves. To stay in tune with just how good it feels to be in the hands of a skilled skincare expert we have to be in those hands ourselves sometimes. It's so easy to forget why customers look forward to our services when we only perform them rather than experience them passively and peacefully. By becoming re-acquainted with the magic of our treatments we'll be refreshed in the full knowledge of what customers hope to feel when they come to us for some of that magic.

Even great chefs are often fans of others who work in their profession.

Give Yourself Some Love

I keep a file of the many written cards and letters clients have sent praising my work and thanking me for the wonderful difference I made in their life and/or in the lives of other family members. Some come as emails and I save those in a special file, too. During darker moments I open these files and remind myself of my work's value to others, something I can't do often enough. Uplifting and reassuring messages like these, ones that took the time and openness of someone's heart to write, will always carry your thoughts back to a more positive perspective. You've earned those kudos so why deny them to yourself? This is the ultimate way to indulge!

Happiness Begins at Home

No one, no words of wisdom or spiritual practice can make you happy. Happiness comes moment-by-moment, lasts for a while and then, without noticing it, we drift to neutral or even unpleasant thoughts and feelings. This happens to everyone so there's nothing wrong with you when your spirits begin to settle downward.

You cannot wish you were happy and be happy at the same time. Wanting will obstruct being. Remember that you're a normal human being, finding your way through a complex and mystifying life... almost all of it by experimentation. In the end we get what we work for the longest time regardless of what it is. But, we can increase our passages of pleasure and coax them to last a little longer when we make it one of our life's purposes. And never forget, when you're happy other people will feel happier because of you. We get what we've got.

<u>NOTES / COMMENTS:</u>

1) What discoveries did you make while reading this chapter?

2) How will you use the information you learned?

3) List 3 things you will do to advance your career.

Some Almost Final Thoughts

Day one of my very first job in skincare began well enough. The salon owners set me up in a little tree-house-like loft perched above the hairstyling floor. It was a beautiful serene setting with lots of clients visiting the hairdressers employed there. What an exciting, thrilling morning! But, by mid-afternoon I had slowly sunk into a silent, doubt-filled panic. I realized that I had no idea how to attract clients to my services, and even barely understood those that I offered.

Being shy and insecure back then, it took all I had to show my face on the salon floor only to feel isolated and in the way when I was there. After a few tense minutes, I wound up creeping back upstairs for lonesome relief. Suddenly my shaded loft seemed more like a prison cell, with me locked inside steadily deteriorating in both morale and outlook.

I tormented myself with questions like: "Did I make a mistake choosing this profession?" "Does anyone really want facial treatments?" "Am I just not right for this kind of business?"

My questions continued on like that, each one driving me lower and more dispirited than the one before. There were no helpful books like this one to offer me encouraging insights and I scarcely knew anyone else in the profession to seek advice from. I almost quit then and there. How glad I am now that I didn't.

Thirty-five plus years later, it's obvious to me now that what I didn't and really couldn't have known back then was due to the lack of experience, time and practice. Mine has been an incredibly educational and rewarding career. It has taught me how to be a better person; one eventually gifted with far more patience and understanding toward others than I was in the beginning.

Years in professional esthetics brought me friendships, love and a satisfying income. It also forced me to grow, mature and learn how to handle difficult problems I once ran away from. A long career in skincare has provided me with years of extremely pleasant employment. Over time I made a respectable name for myself in the esthetics industry and contributed meaningful assistance to those coming up after me; people who have the same responsibility toward caring for clients that I had and have still. I can't imagine anything else I would rather have done with my working life.

Looking Ahead

We truly are limited only by our ability to imagine and the drive to put that imagination into practice. Professional esthetics can seem like such a small opportunity from the viewpoint of a confined treatment room. After waxing your five-hundredth leg you might feel as though you've rounded that routine one too many times. No one could blame you for feeling that way, but remaining stuck in those feelings is a daily decision that can be changed into something better if you want to. There are many good reasons to improve our career outlook:

- Even though beauty schools are churning out new estheticians at a machine-like rate, most of them will abandon the profession in short time, leaving more opportunity for those who stick with the career.
- While technology and product formulations are advancing rapidly you have no reason to worry knowing that most facial clients are still primarily seeking a relief from daily stress during their treatment.
- No online program or mechanical device can ever duplicate or replace what you do that customers love.
- The greatest skills in professional skincare are still patience, consistency and client empathy.
- Age only enhances your esthetics career: you can't trade youthful looks for experience. Customer confidence in you is everything and your age can elevate that.
- You can receive a pay raise every day just by challenging yourself to work more effectively with every client. Not every professional can do that, especially those who work in salaried positions.
- You might be told how wonderful you are all day long!

120

Some years ago I met an older esthetician who wanted to retire after more than 38 years in the profession. She asked me if I would be interested in buying her practice. This woman sounded tired, worn out and finally ready to put down her tools and smock. She glumly told me that she had had enough of customers and the troubles of managing a business. "I have done all I can for people who don't appreciate me," she said. "I want out now."

Her statement saddened me as she described her years in skincare as a hard personal sacrifice, working with ungrateful clients who failed to bestow whatever level of praise she believed she deserved. The career she portrayed seemed like a waste.

My own experience in the esthetics profession has been anything but years of disappointment and dissatisfaction. It's been a wonder, a miracle, and a gift. I have never allowed anything to discolor my feelings about what I do even when the going wasn't easy. Never. Nor should you. Our careers can be whatever we want them to be.

I hope this book has helped you to feel more confident about your profession and has shed some light on how you might make the most of what it has to offer. You deserve to be whatever you put your heart into, especially when your work helps others look and feel better about themselves inside as well as on the outside.

There's so much ahead for anyone who desires to have a great career in esthetics, including you! Stay with it. Learn from the hard stuff, and work to make your dreams real.

Thanks for buying this book,

Douglas Preston

Esthetician Career Mentoring by Preston

Have you discovered that building a successful career in professional esthetics has been tougher or is taking longer than you expected? You're not alone.

Beauty schools cannot fully prepare students for the difficult challenges of self-employment or practice growth. Your esthetician's license is only the beginning step of a long climb to success and security.

Many professional skincare product companies may generally provide useful education, but none offer you the specific tools to achieve your own personal career goals.

If you are looking for reliable advice for growing a thriving skincare or spa business, you've found the right resource. Whether you are a solo practicing Esthetician, planning to become one, or an employer of an esthetics team, Douglas Preston has methods that will guide your career in the right direction.

Please check out our easy-to-use business coaching plans by visiting https://www.prestonskincenter.com/skin-care-professionals. We offer a FREE initial consultation whereby we can learn about your desires and goals to see how our services may help you reach your dreams. We also have a large list of educational training classes available for online learning in our store: https://www.prestonskincenter.com/consulting-store

Our business advice is designed to be easy for you to follow and respects your limited time and budget. What matters most is that you advance and learn at your own pace while enjoying the benefits of new and proven practice management methods.There's no need to go it alone when you can have a vast source of career information available for your specific needs! Preston welcomes you to write him directly: info@prestonestheticsandconsulting.com